PICTURE BOOK OF
BUTTERFLIES

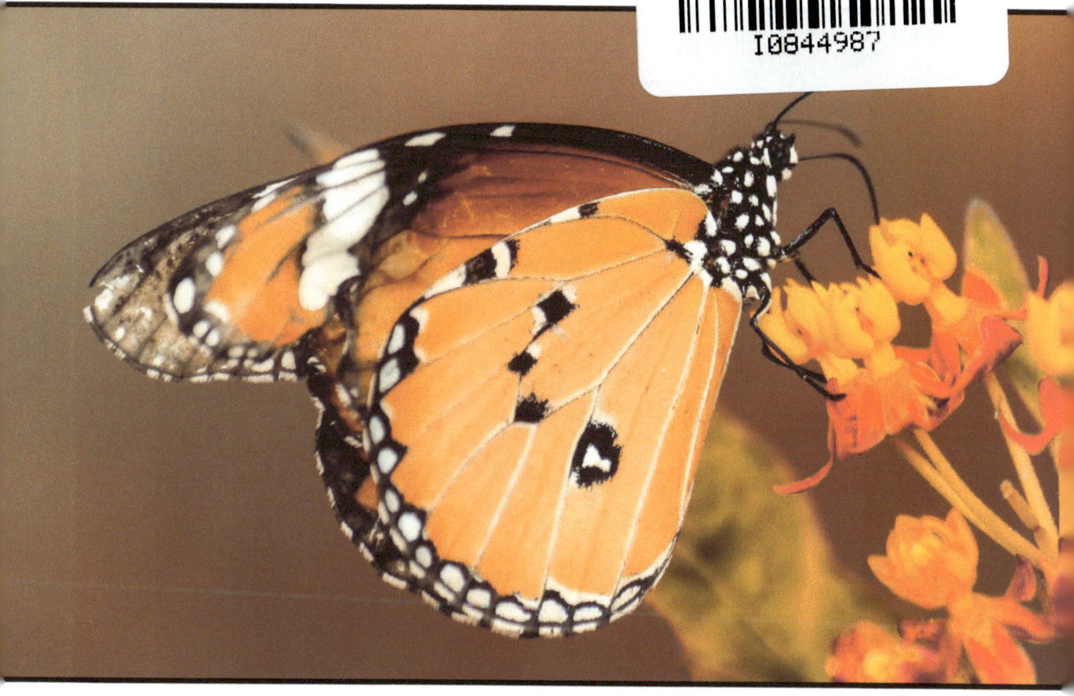

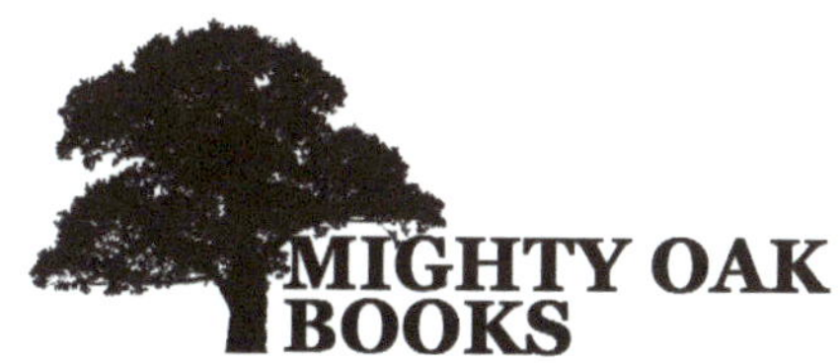

MIGHTY OAK
BOOKS

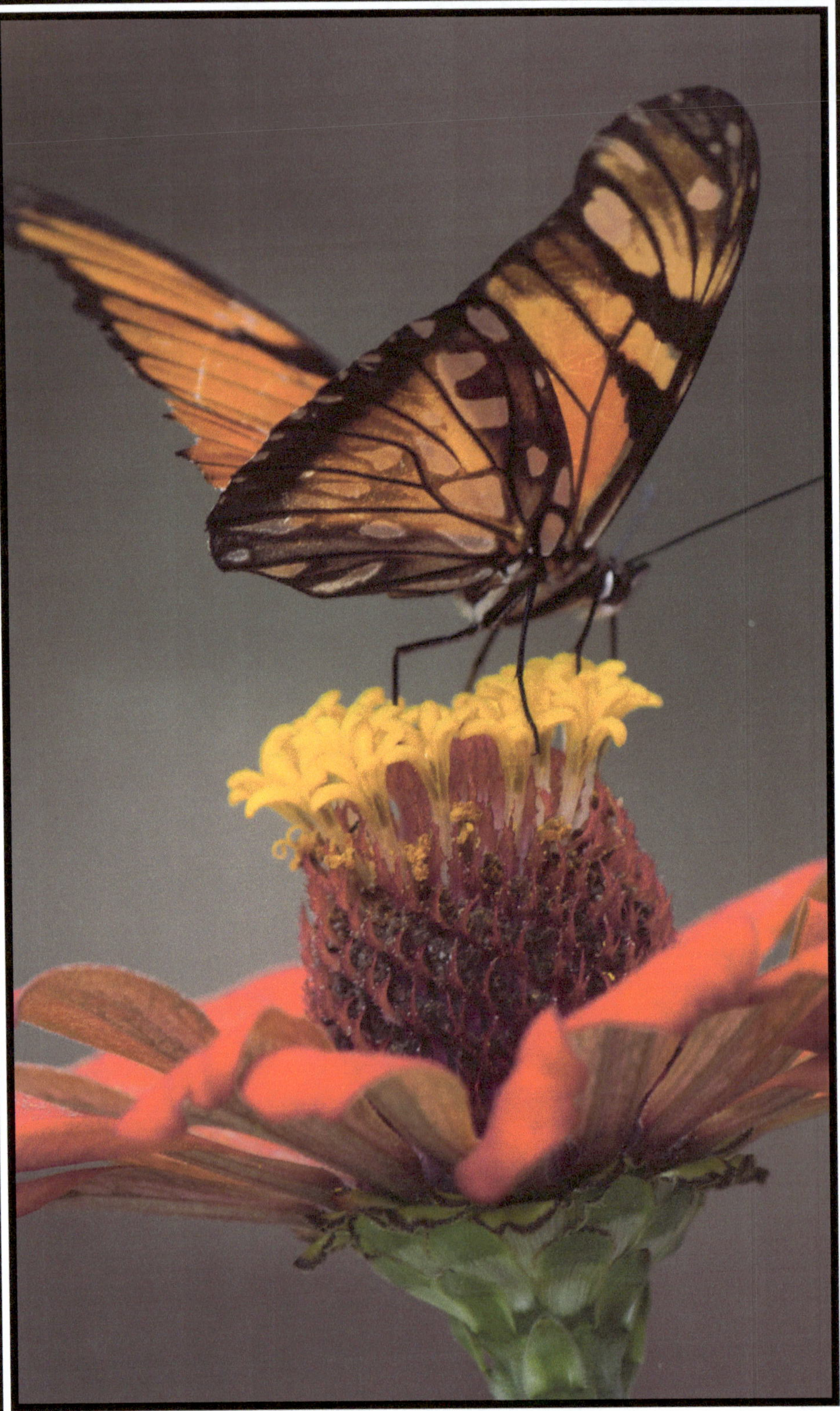

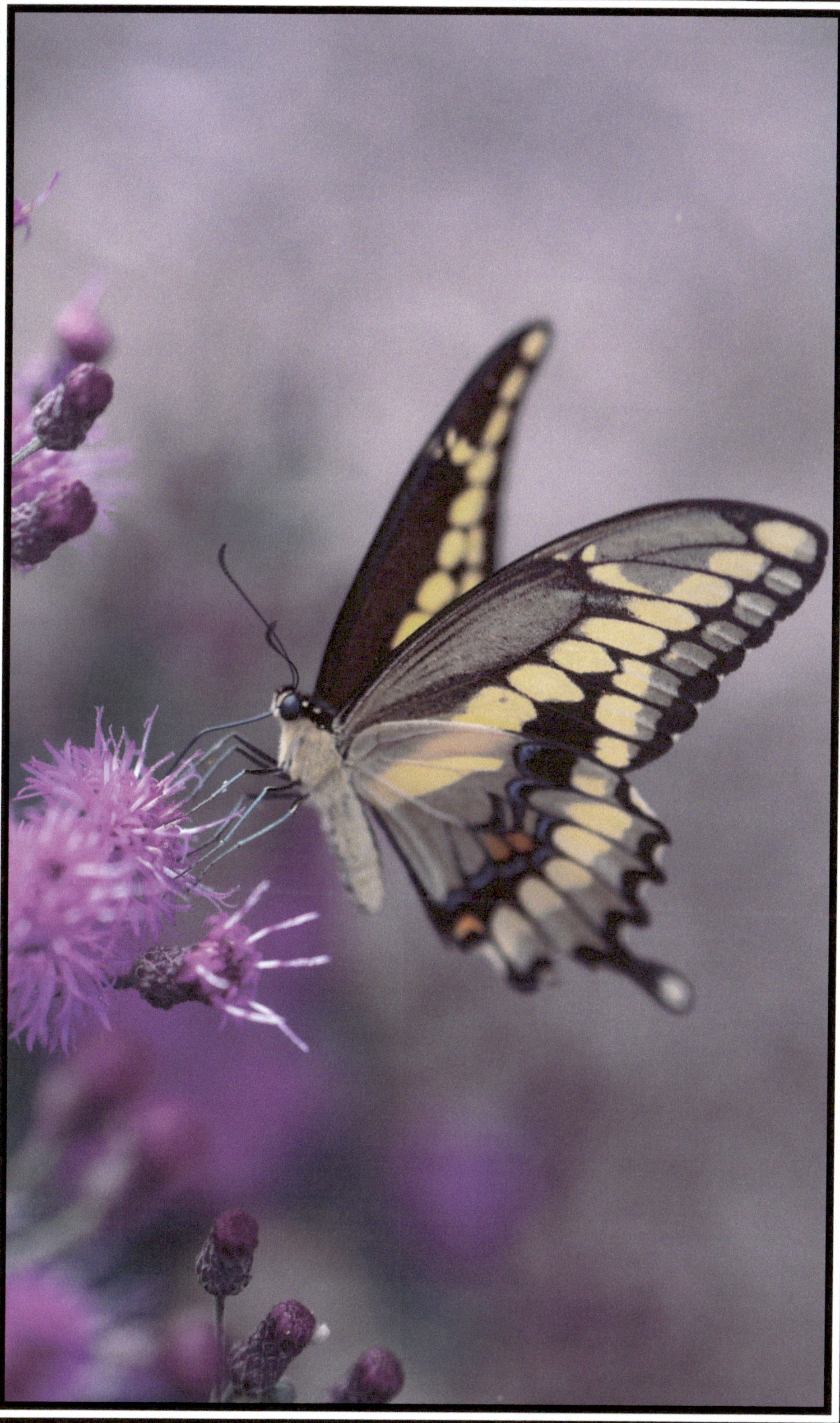

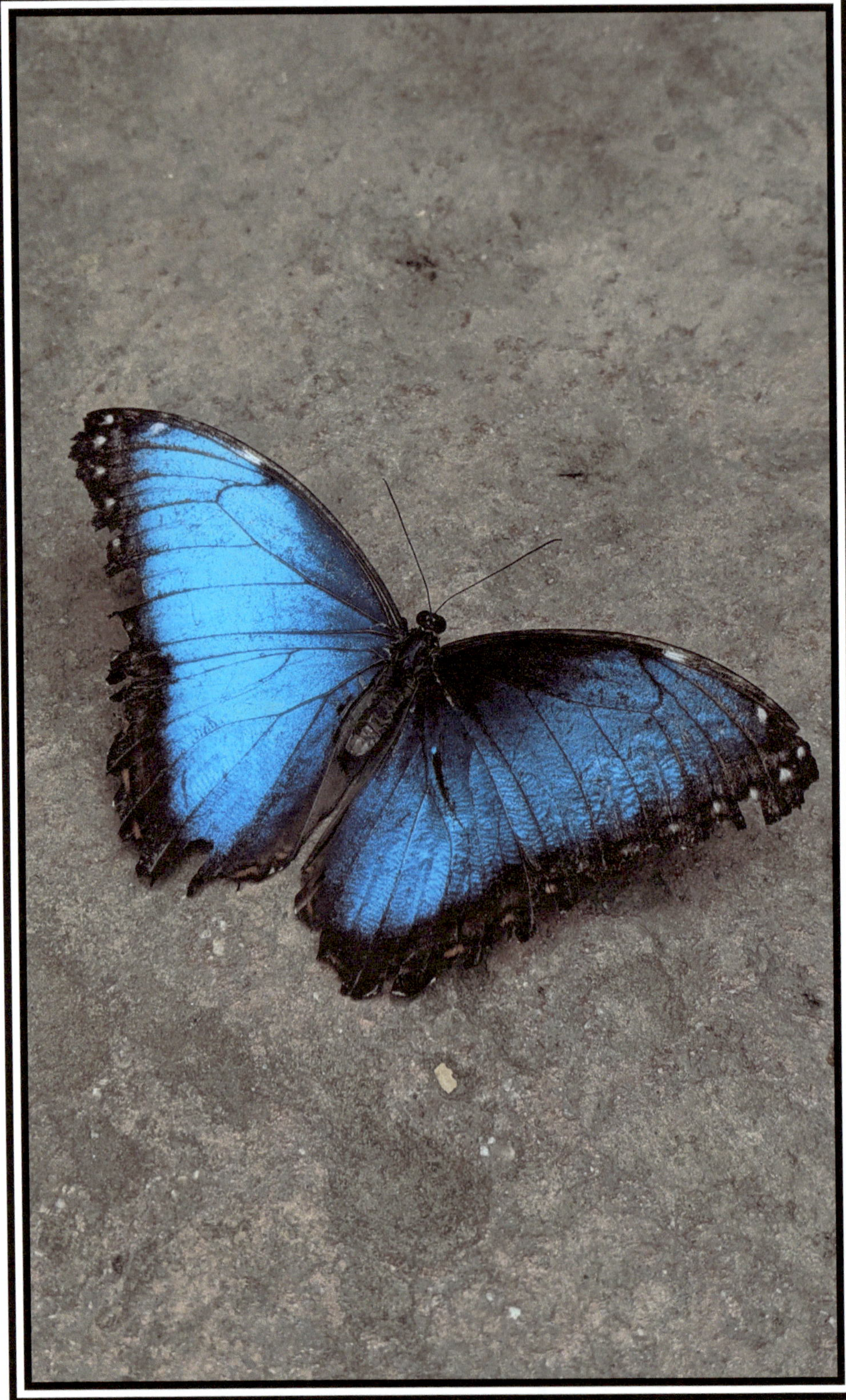

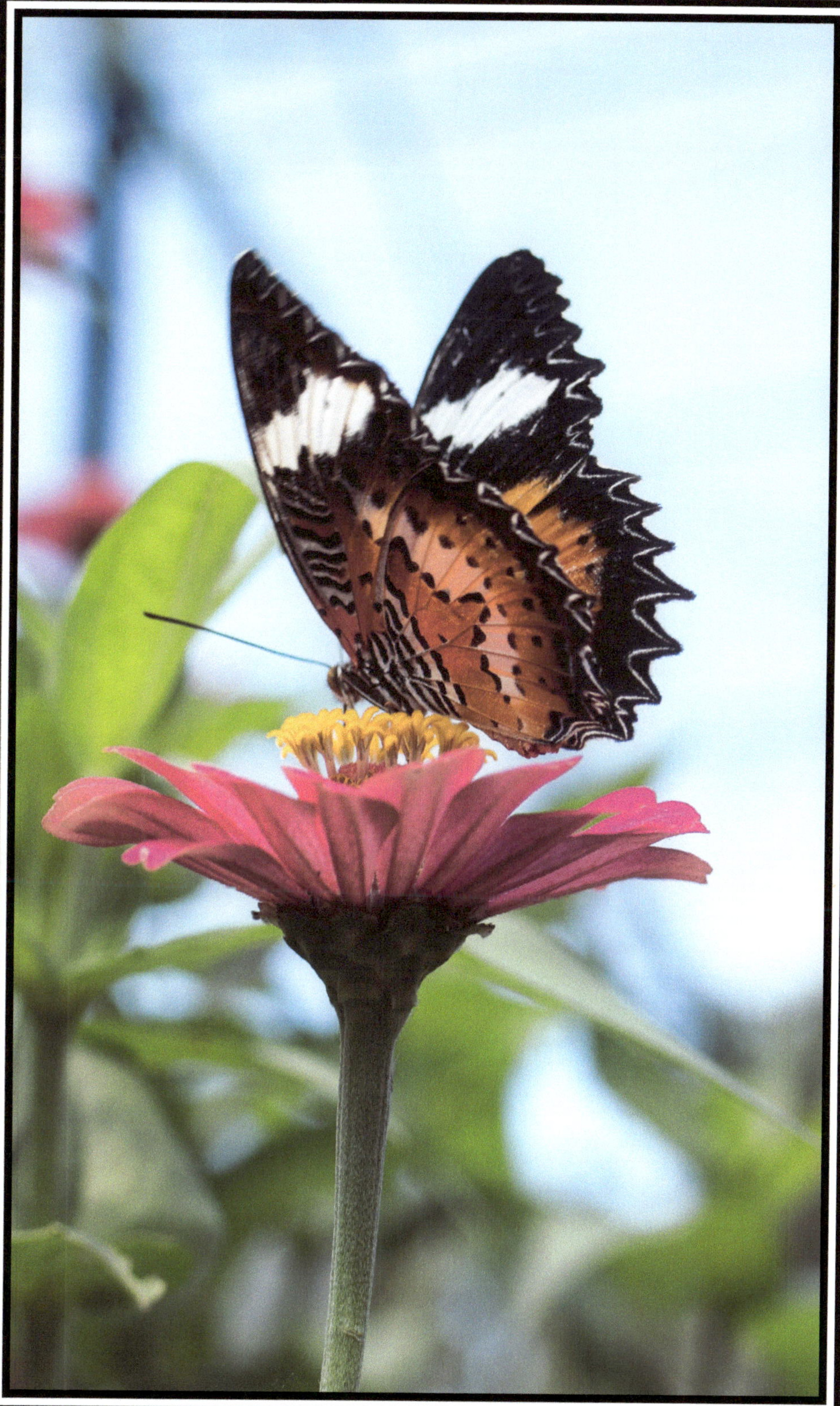

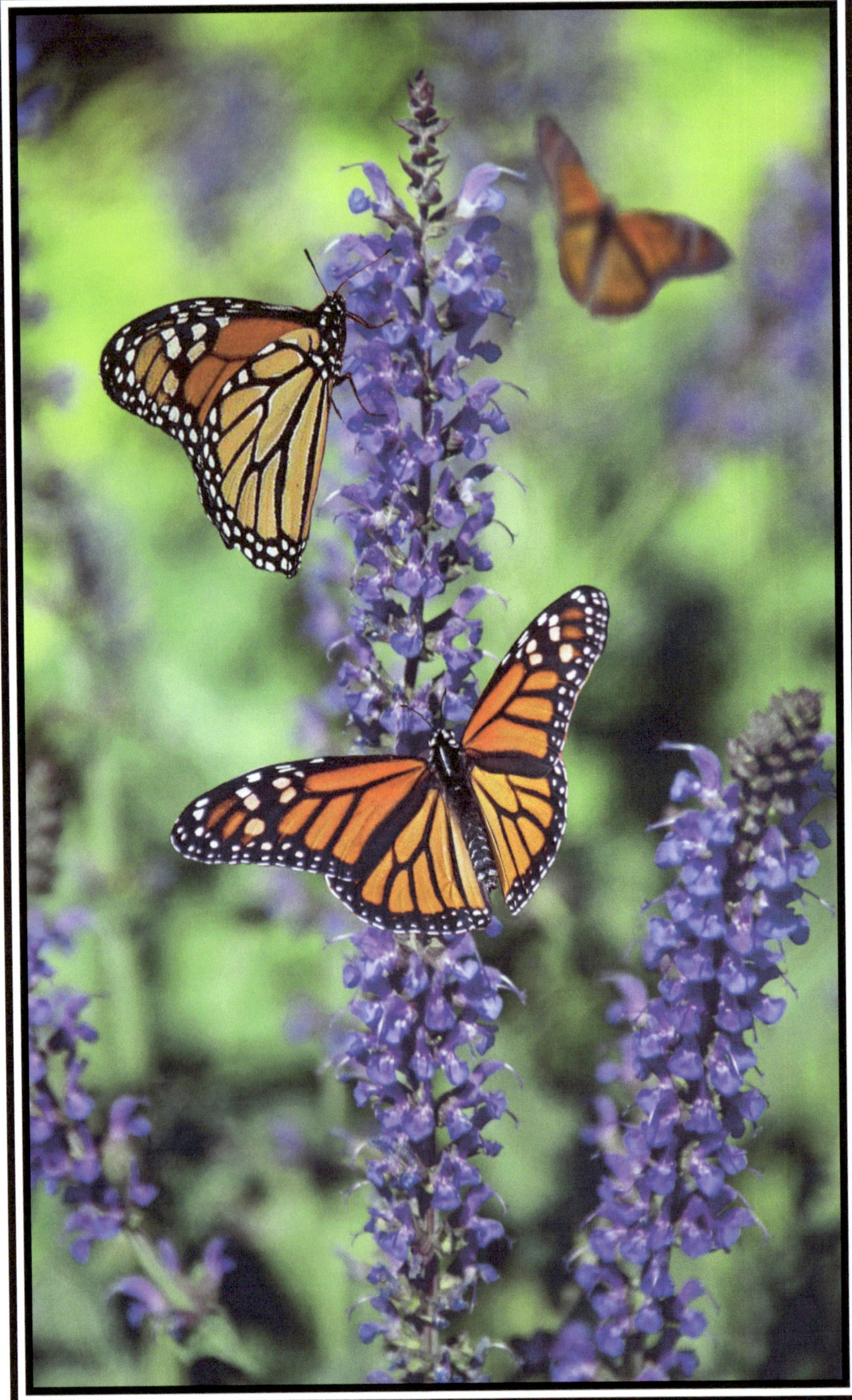

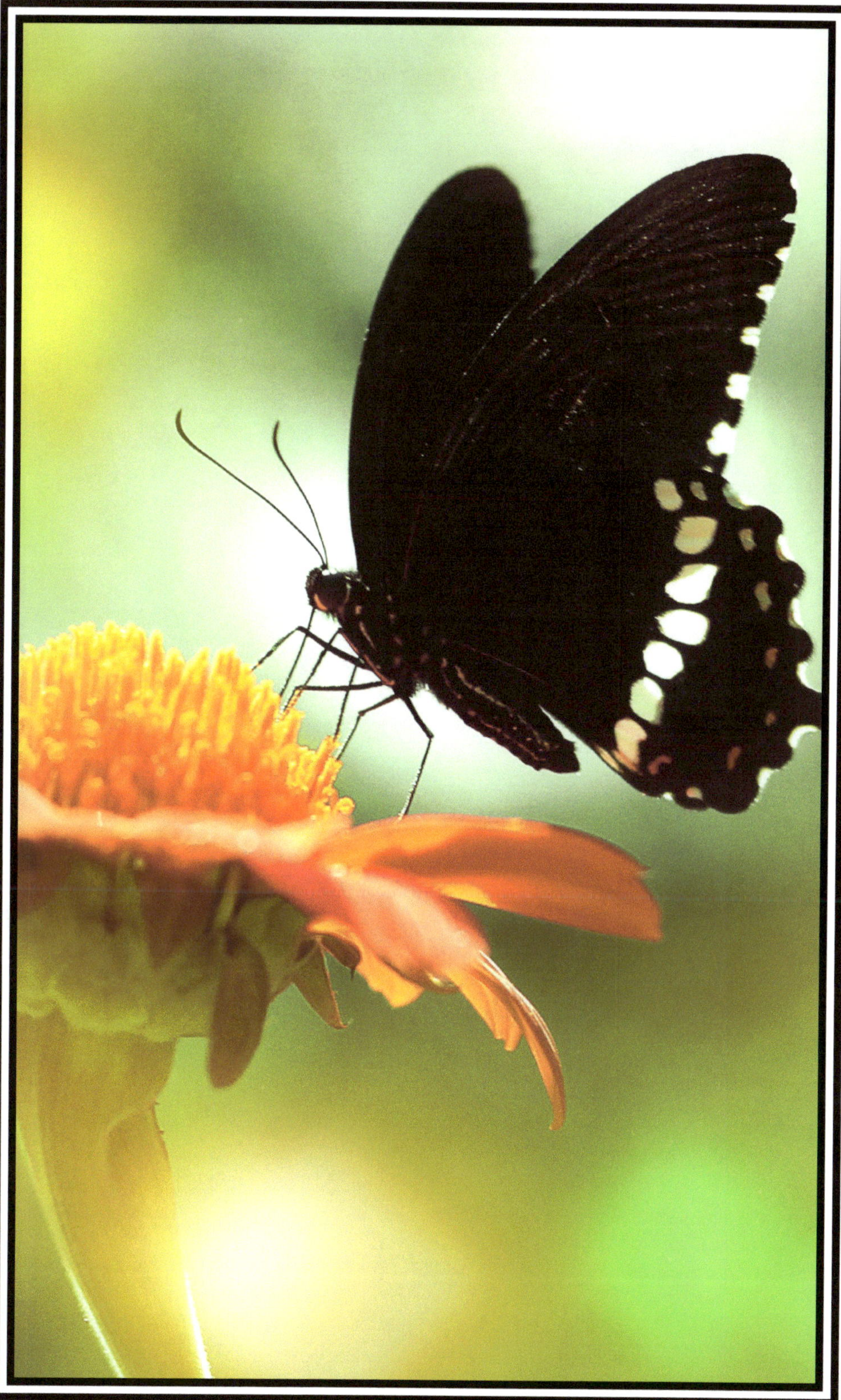

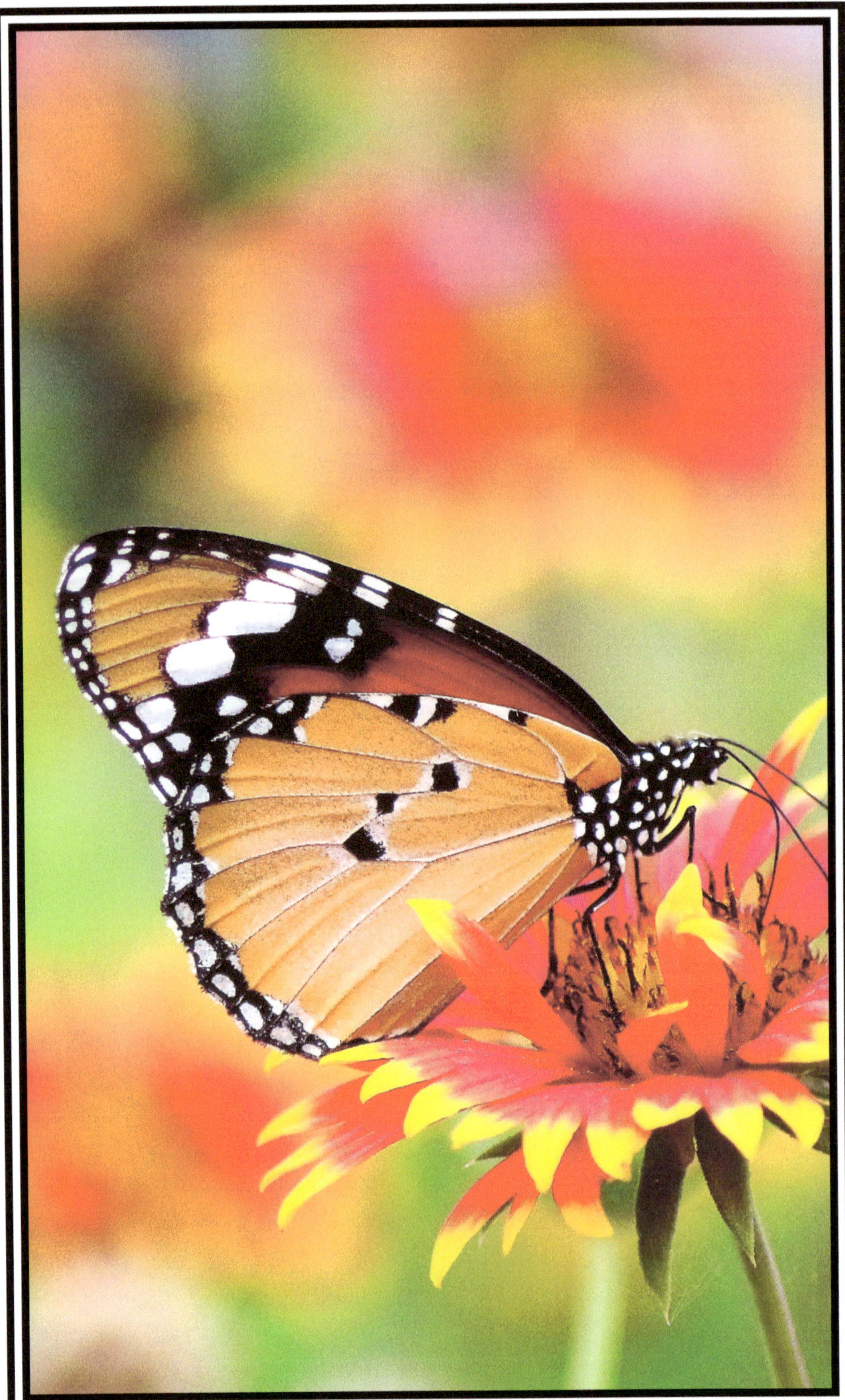

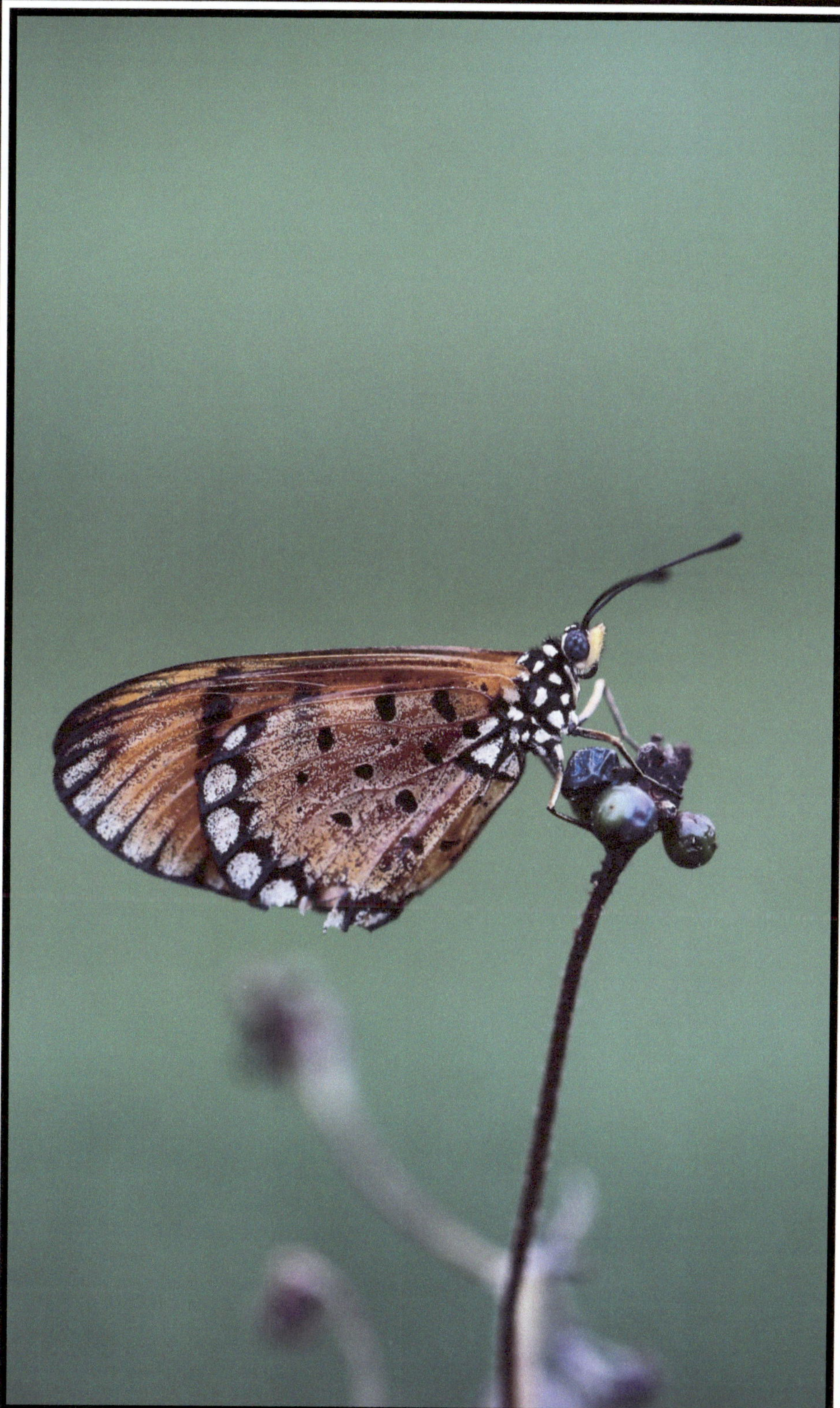

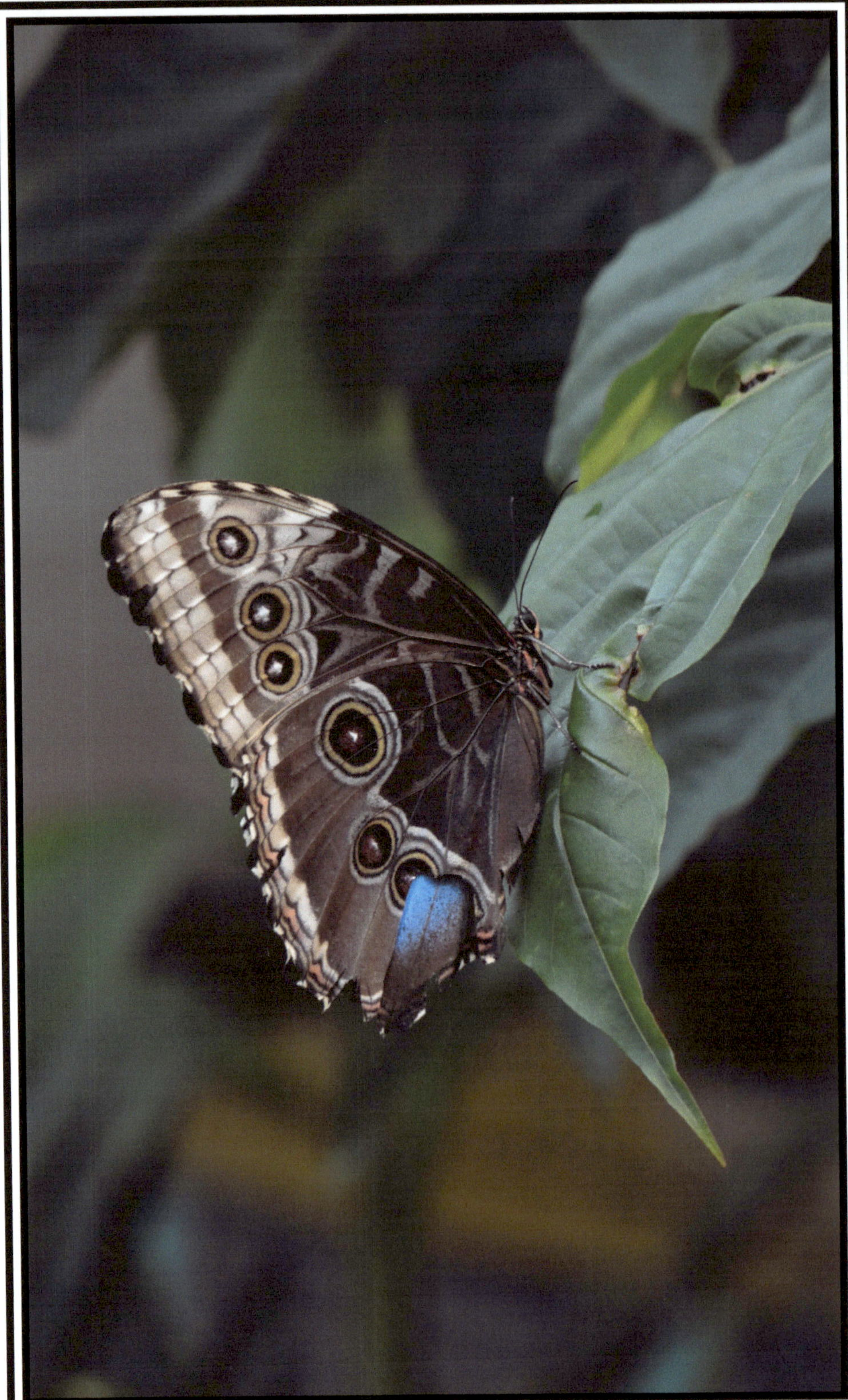

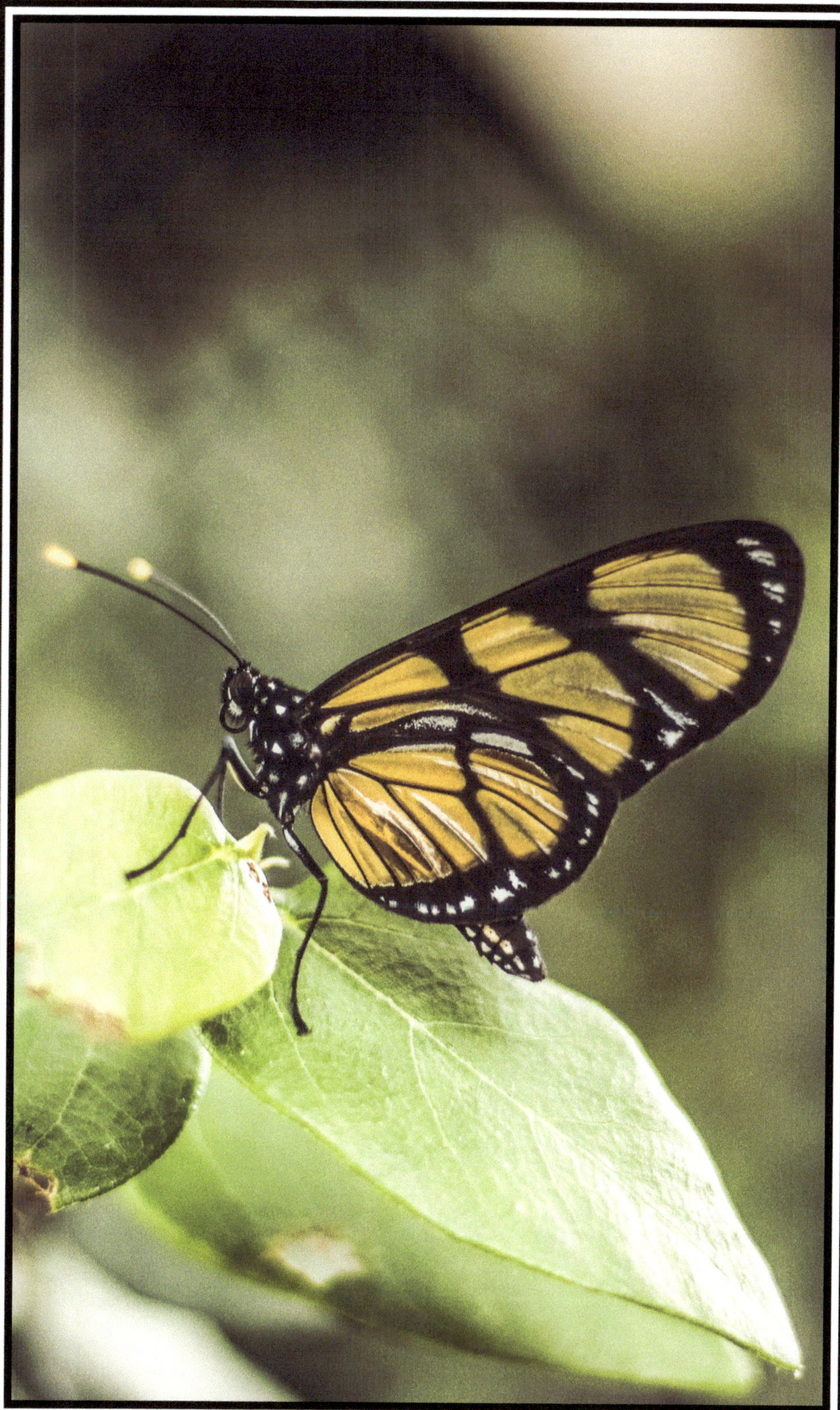

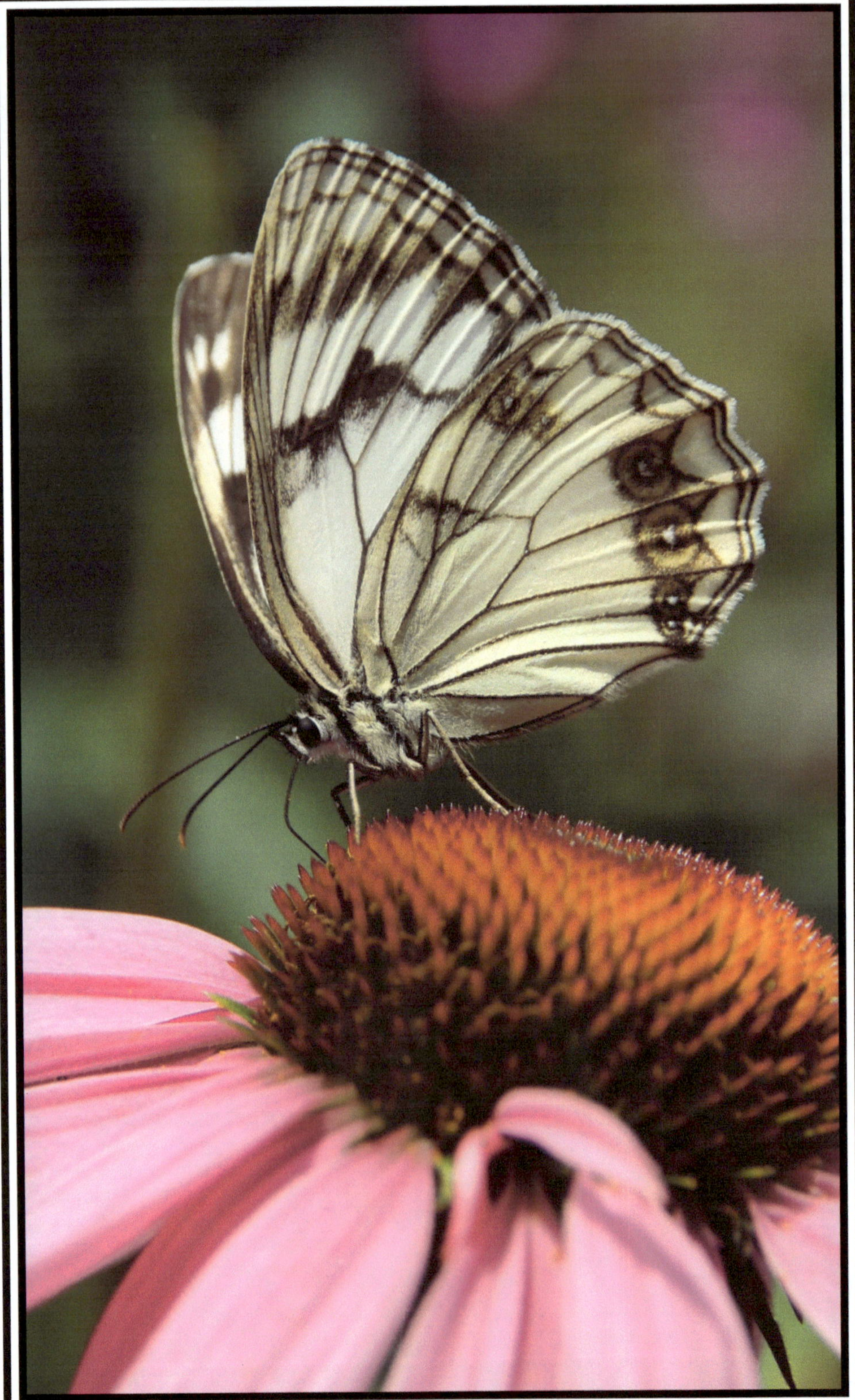

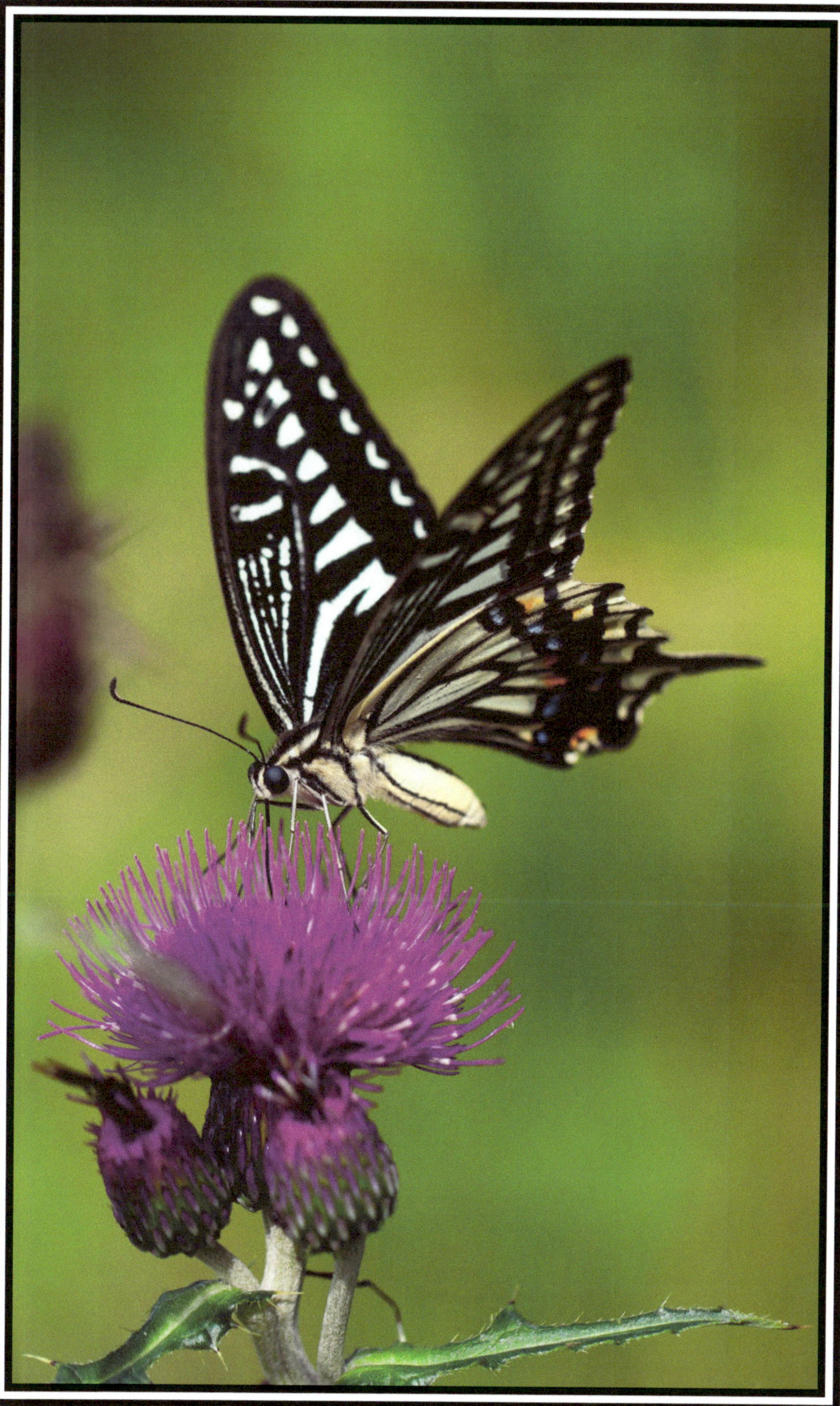

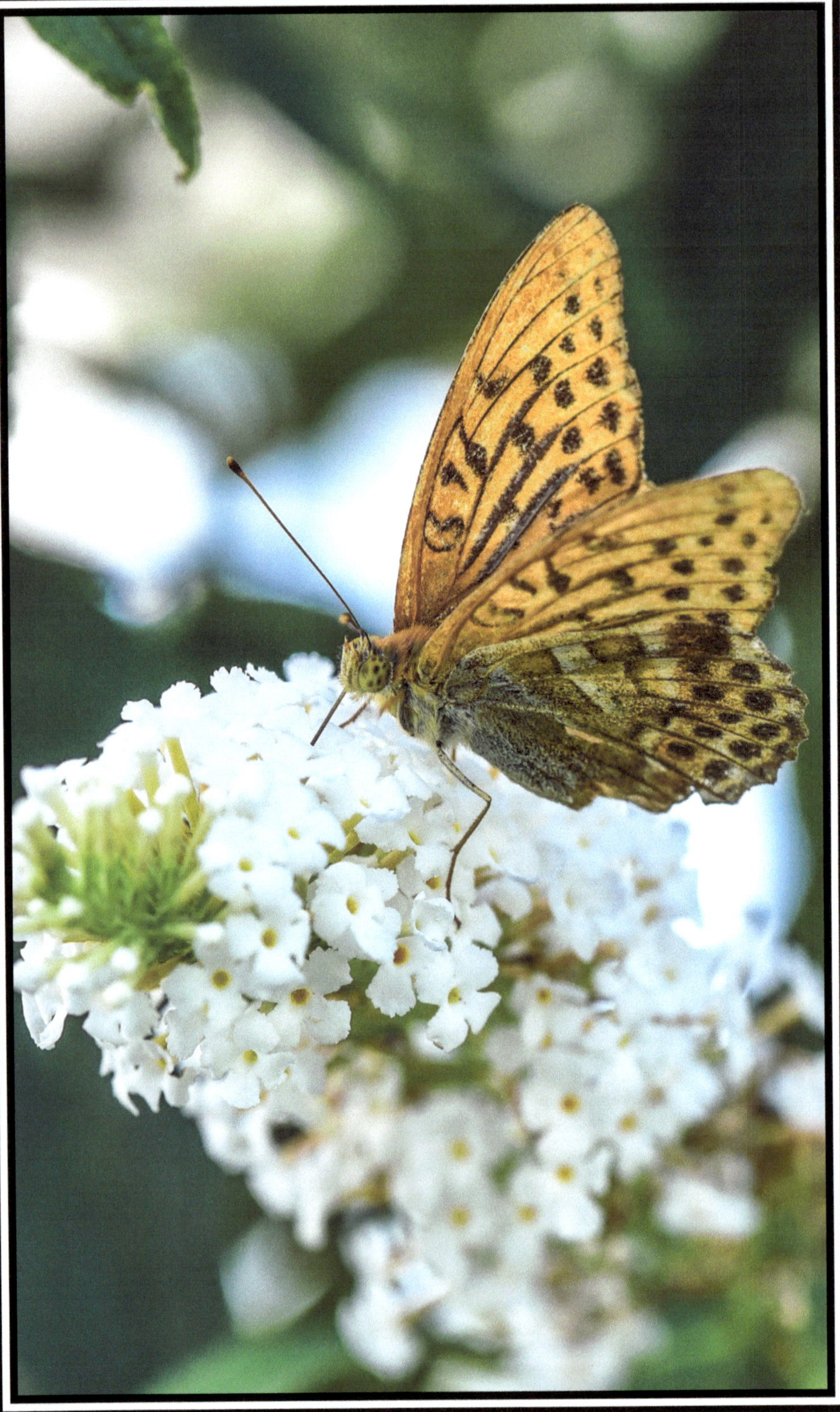

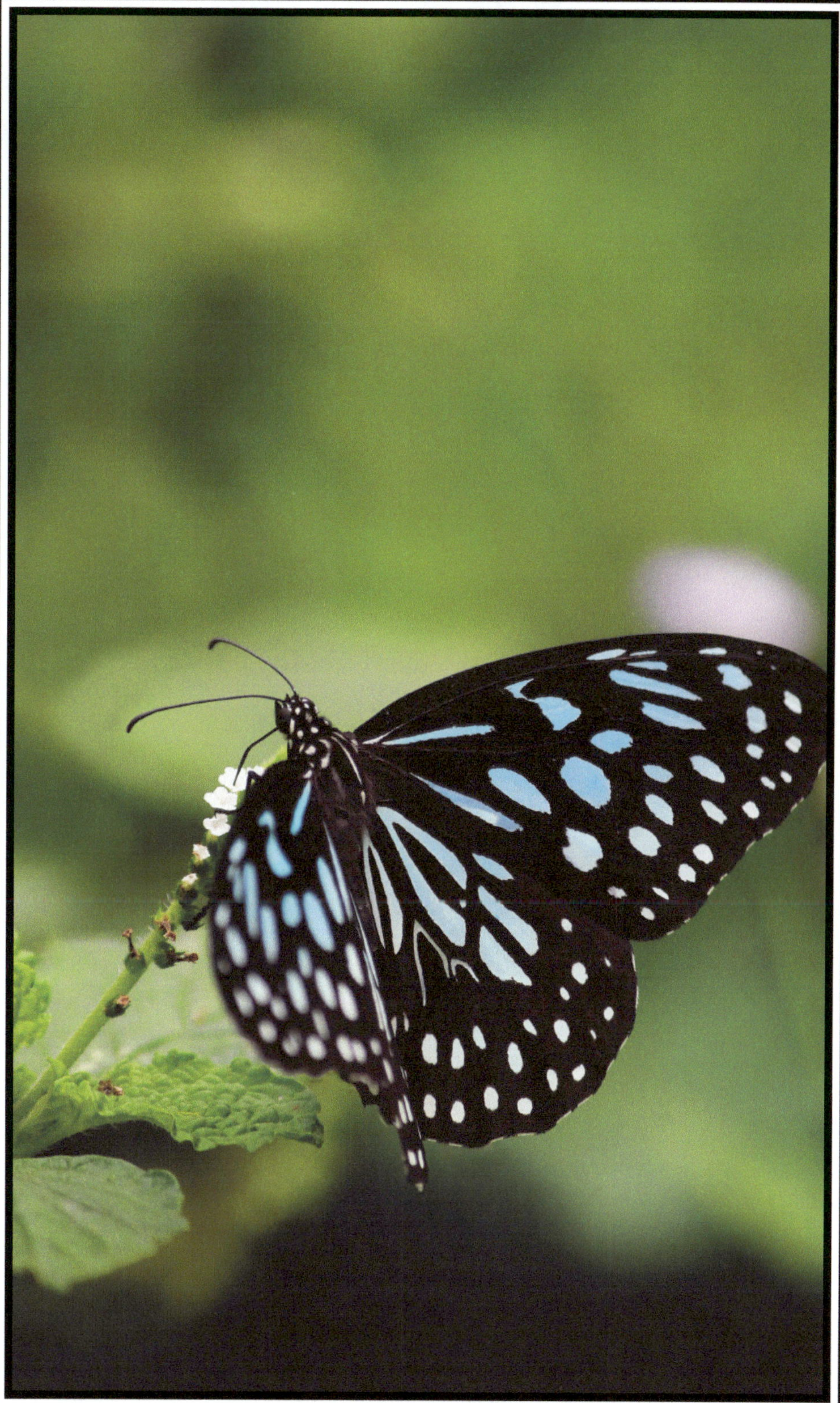

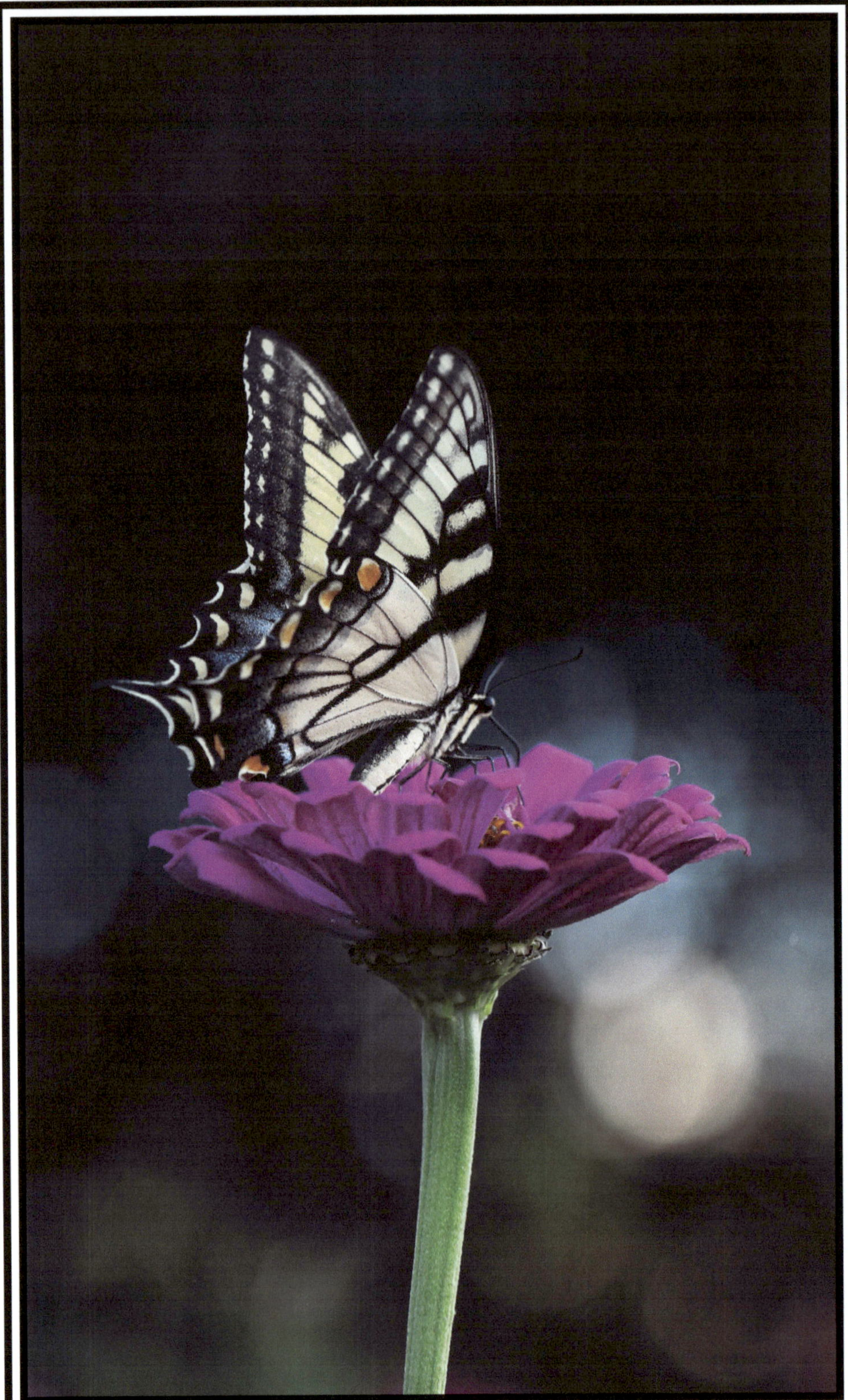

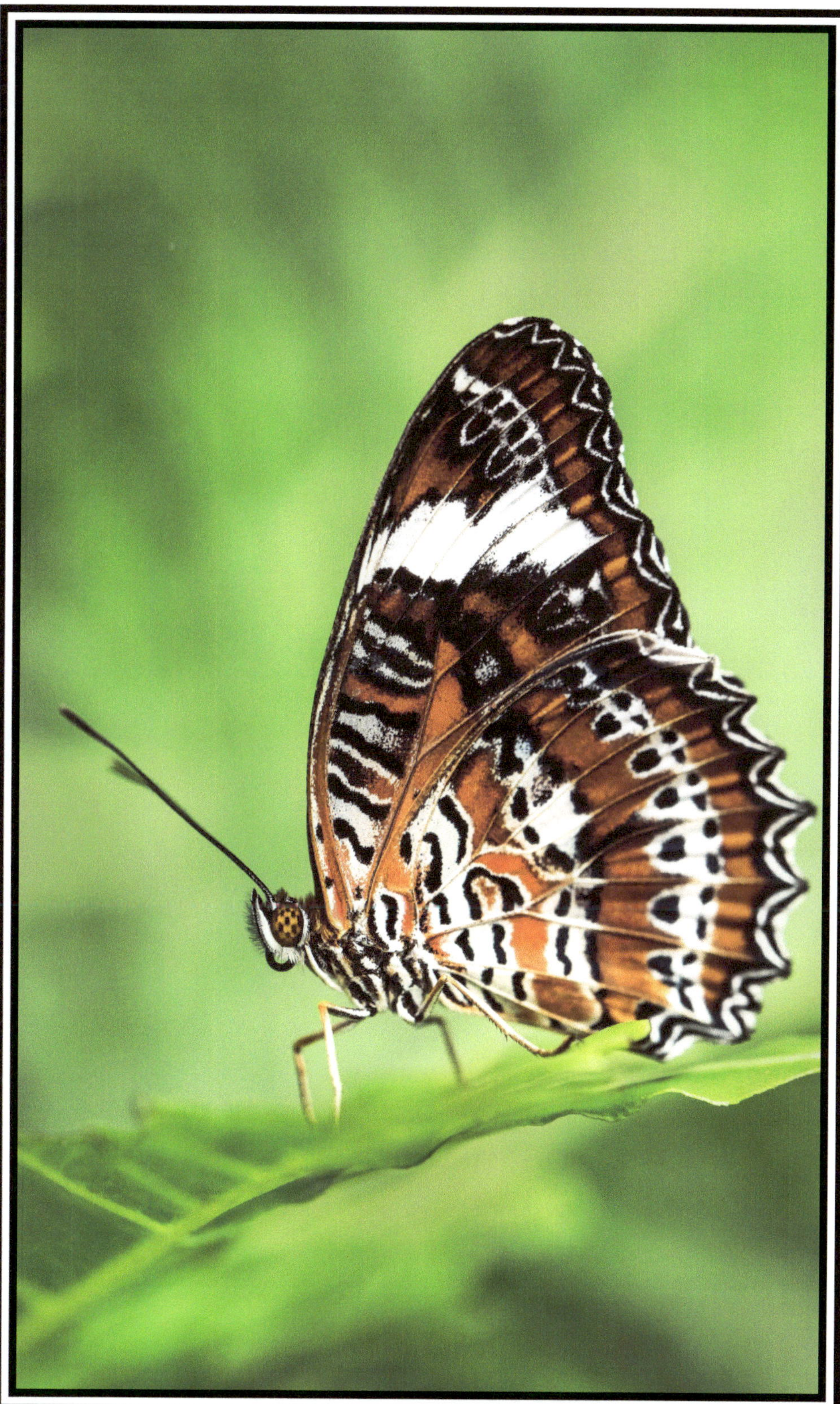

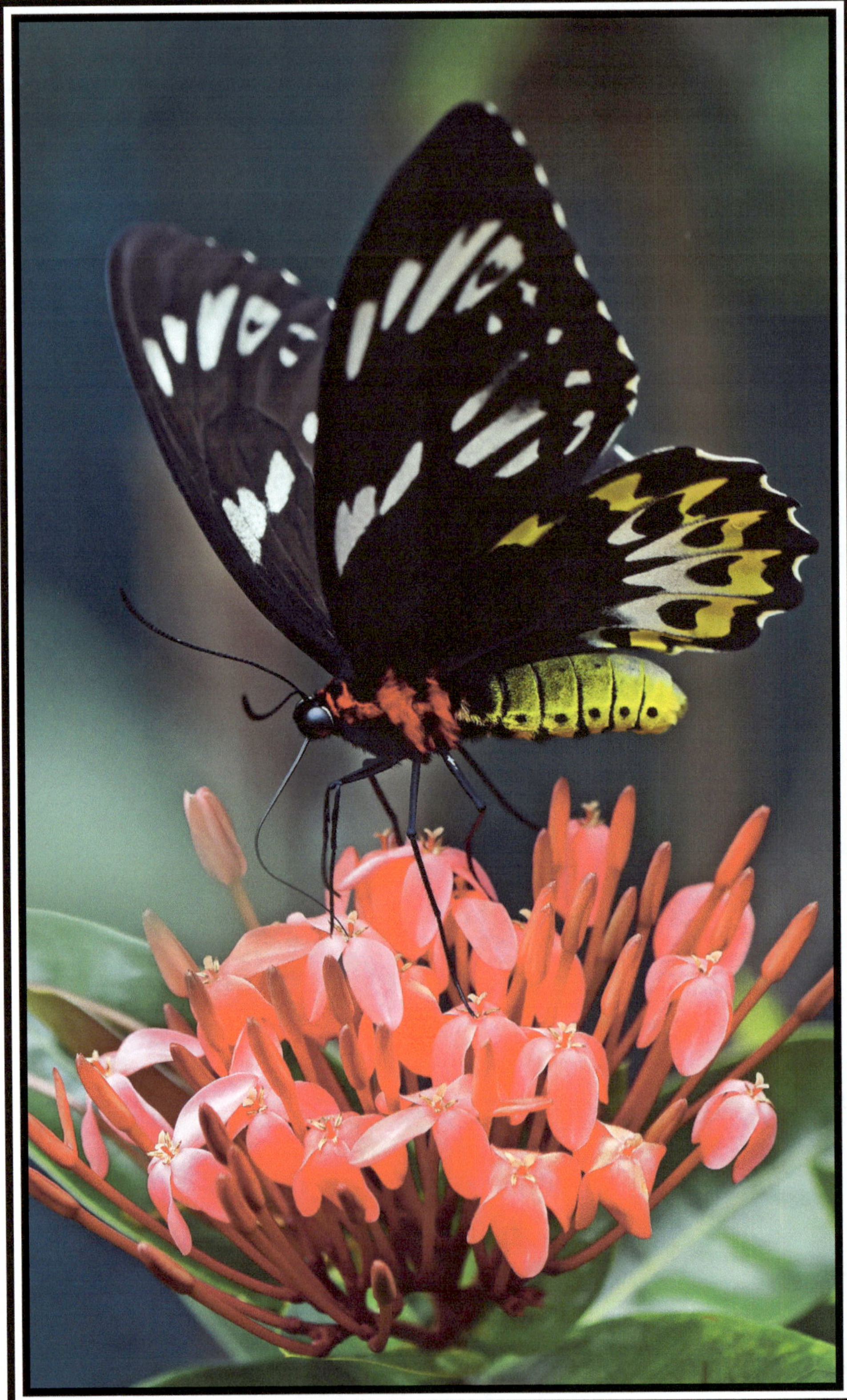

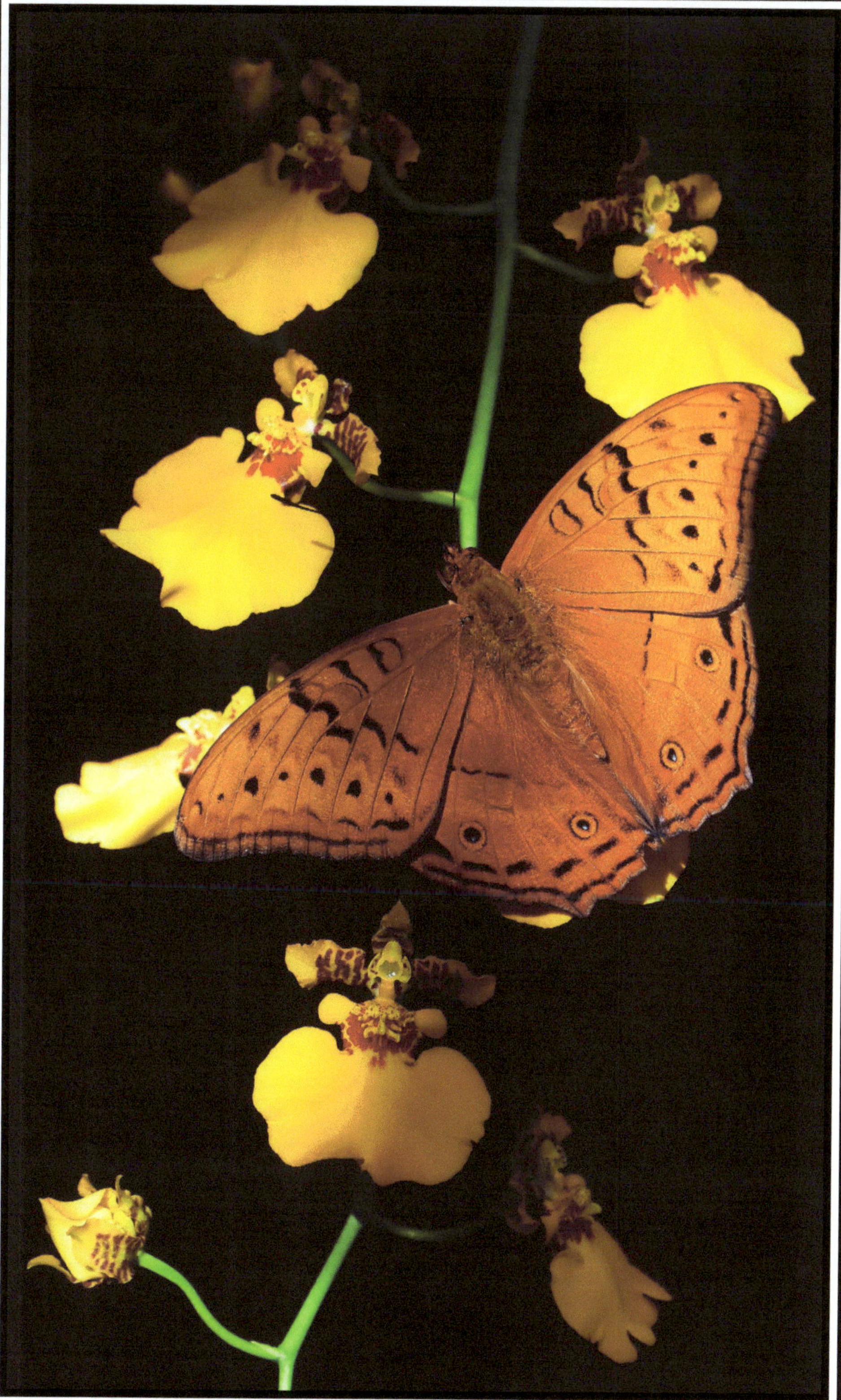

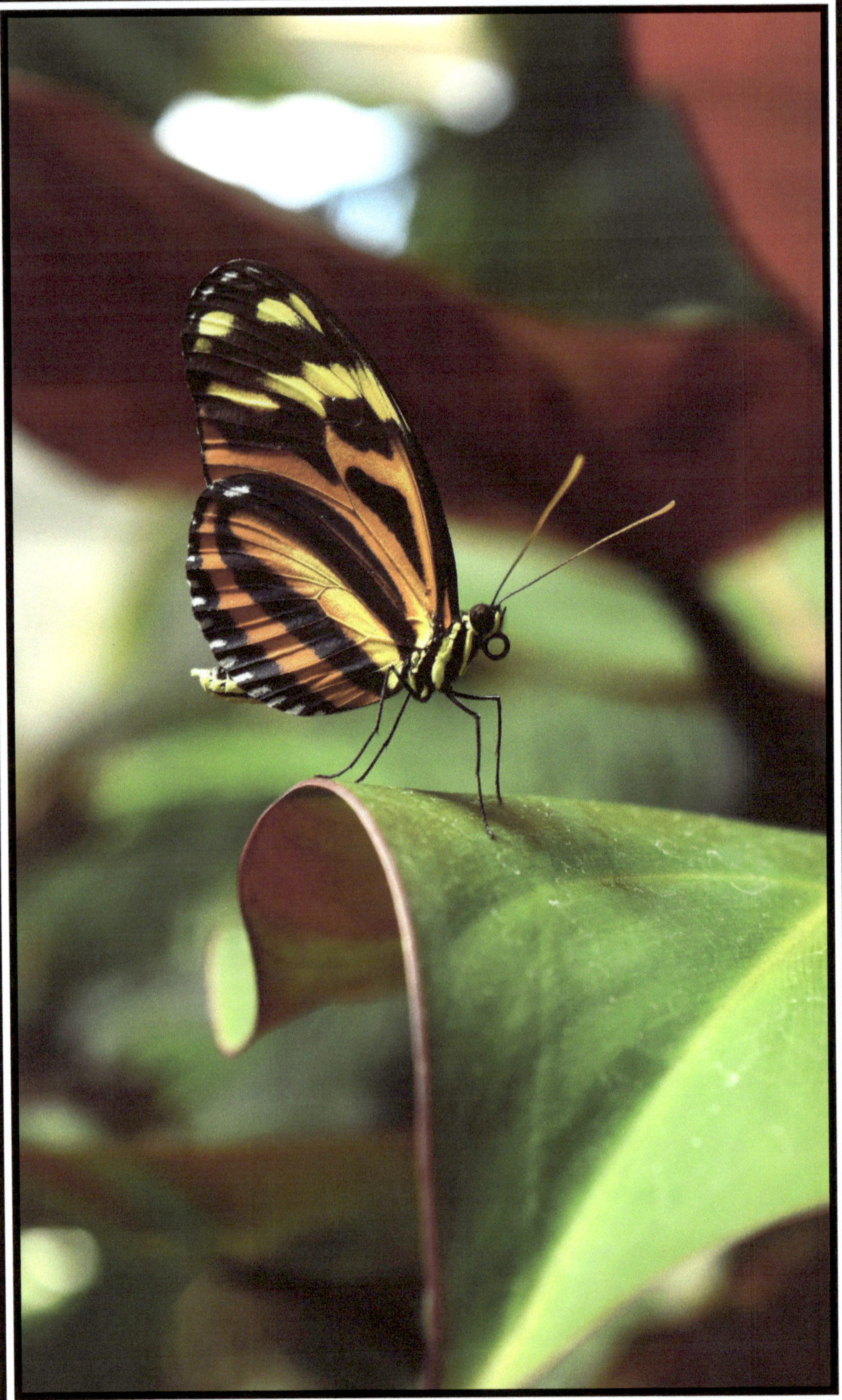

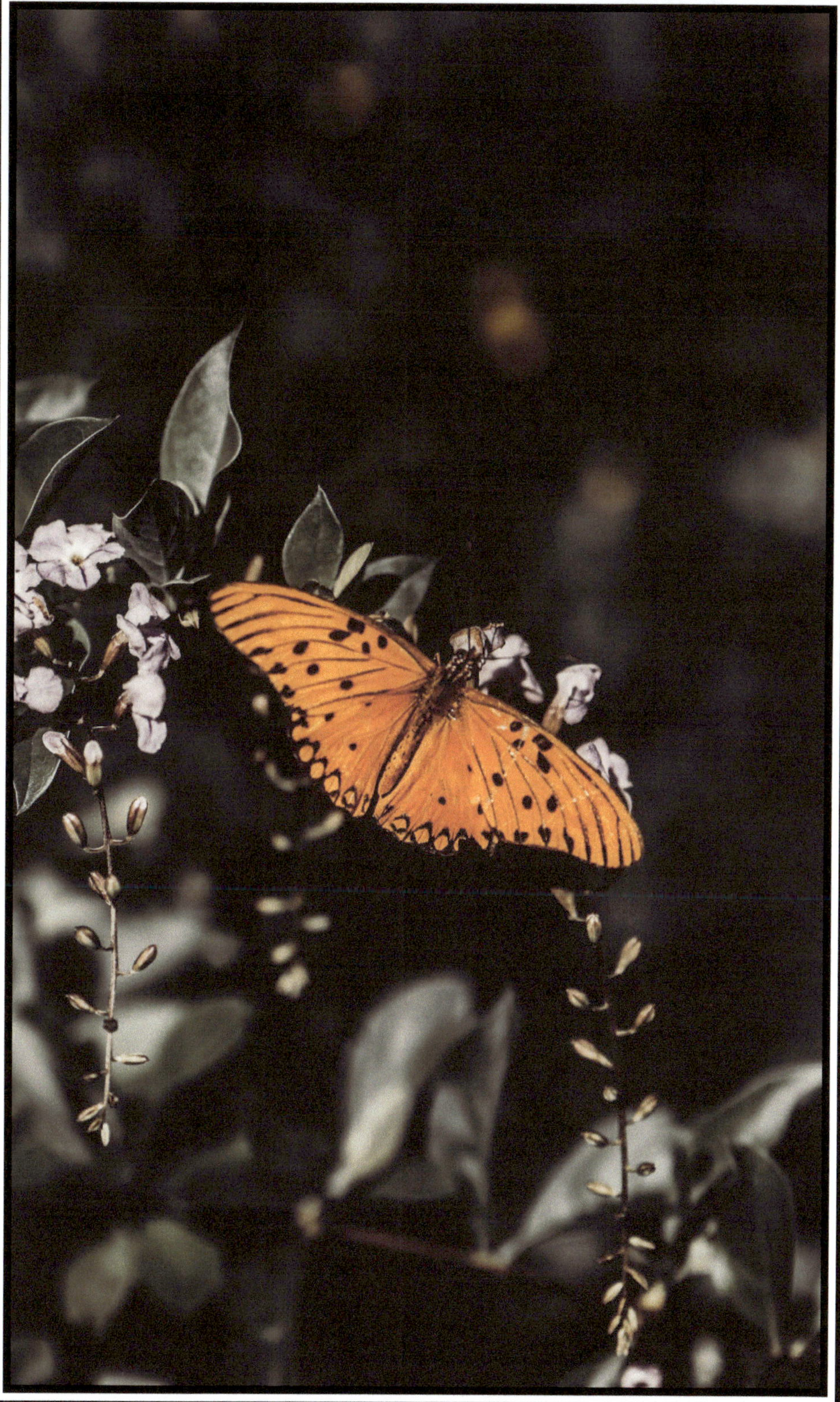

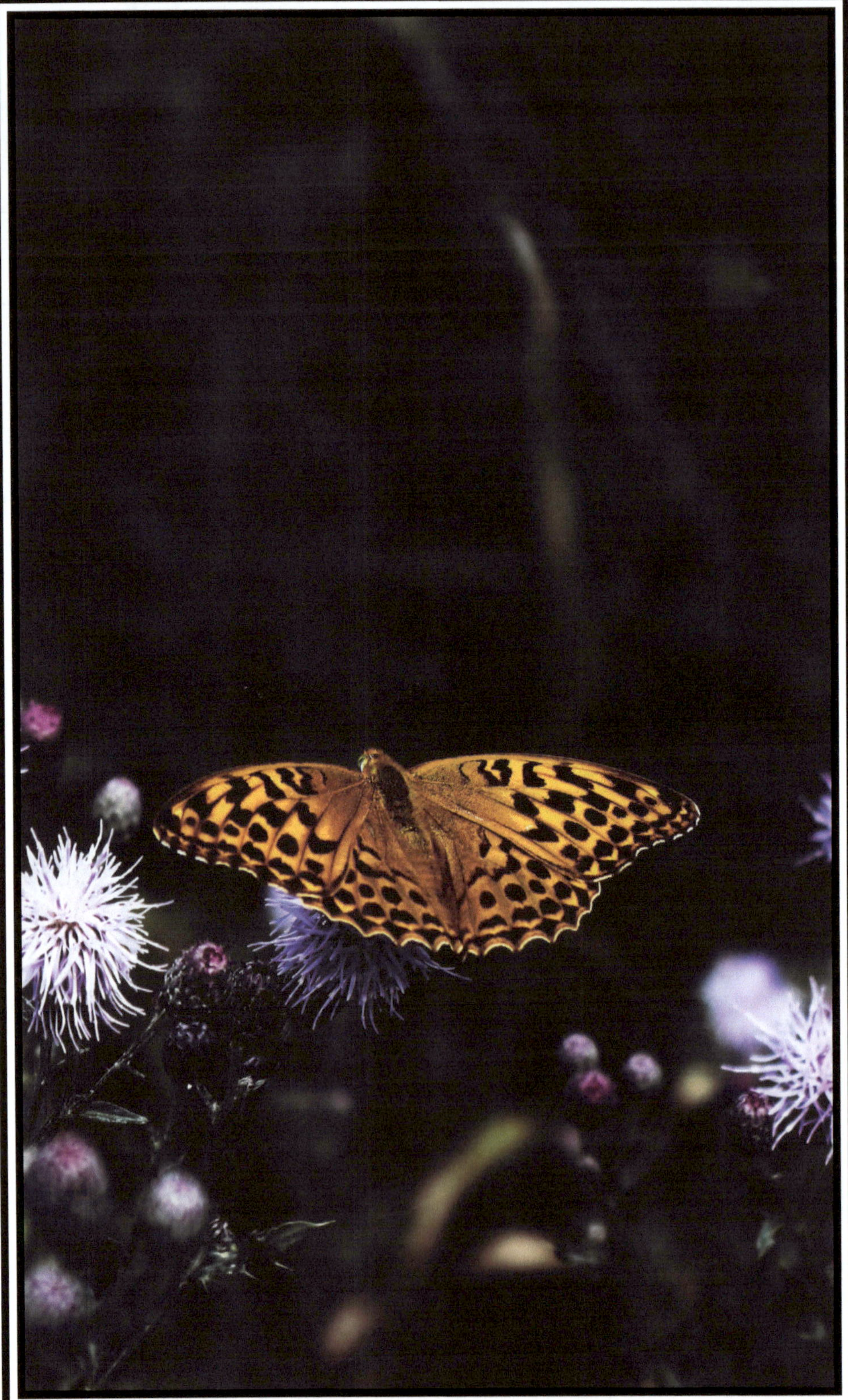

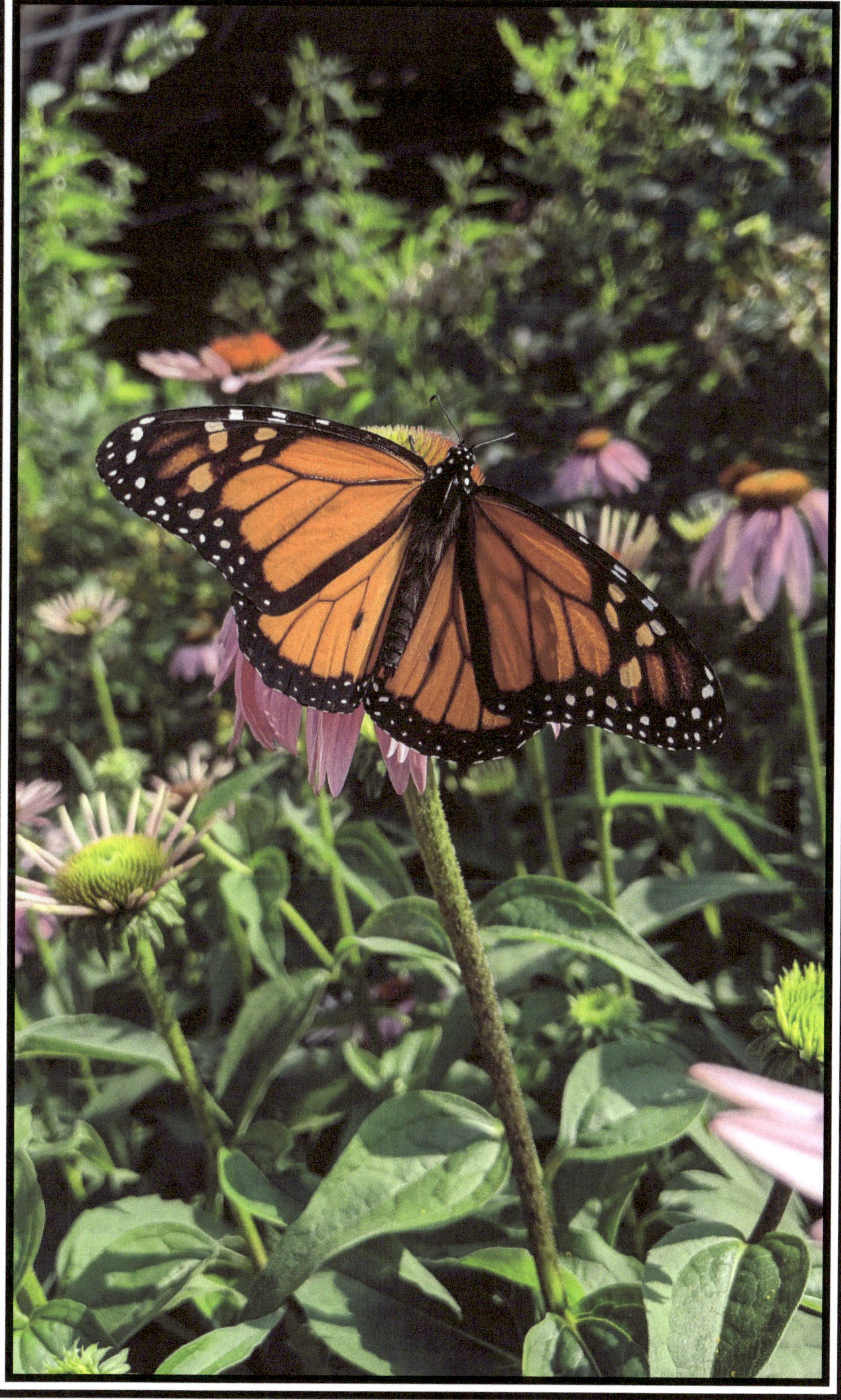

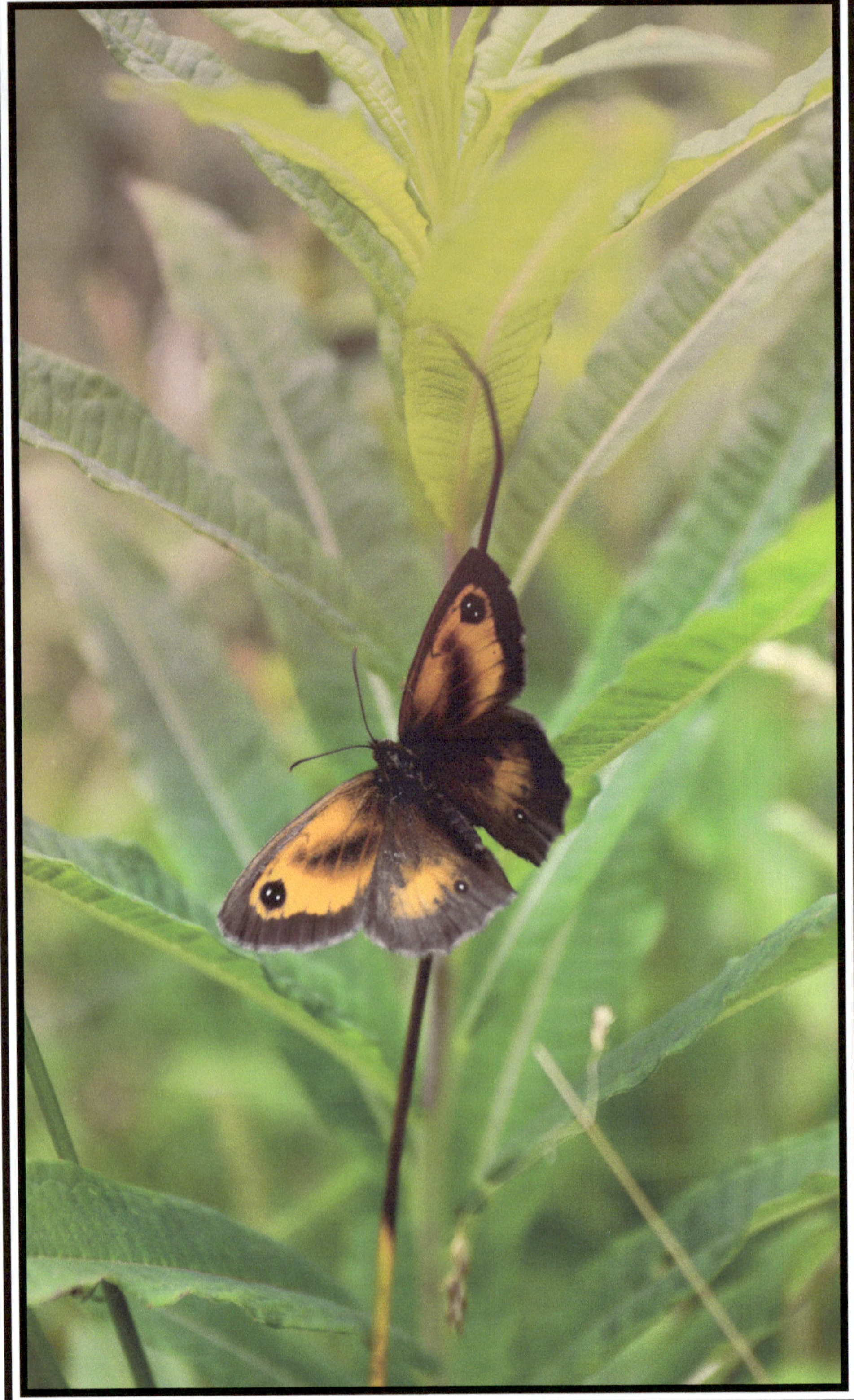

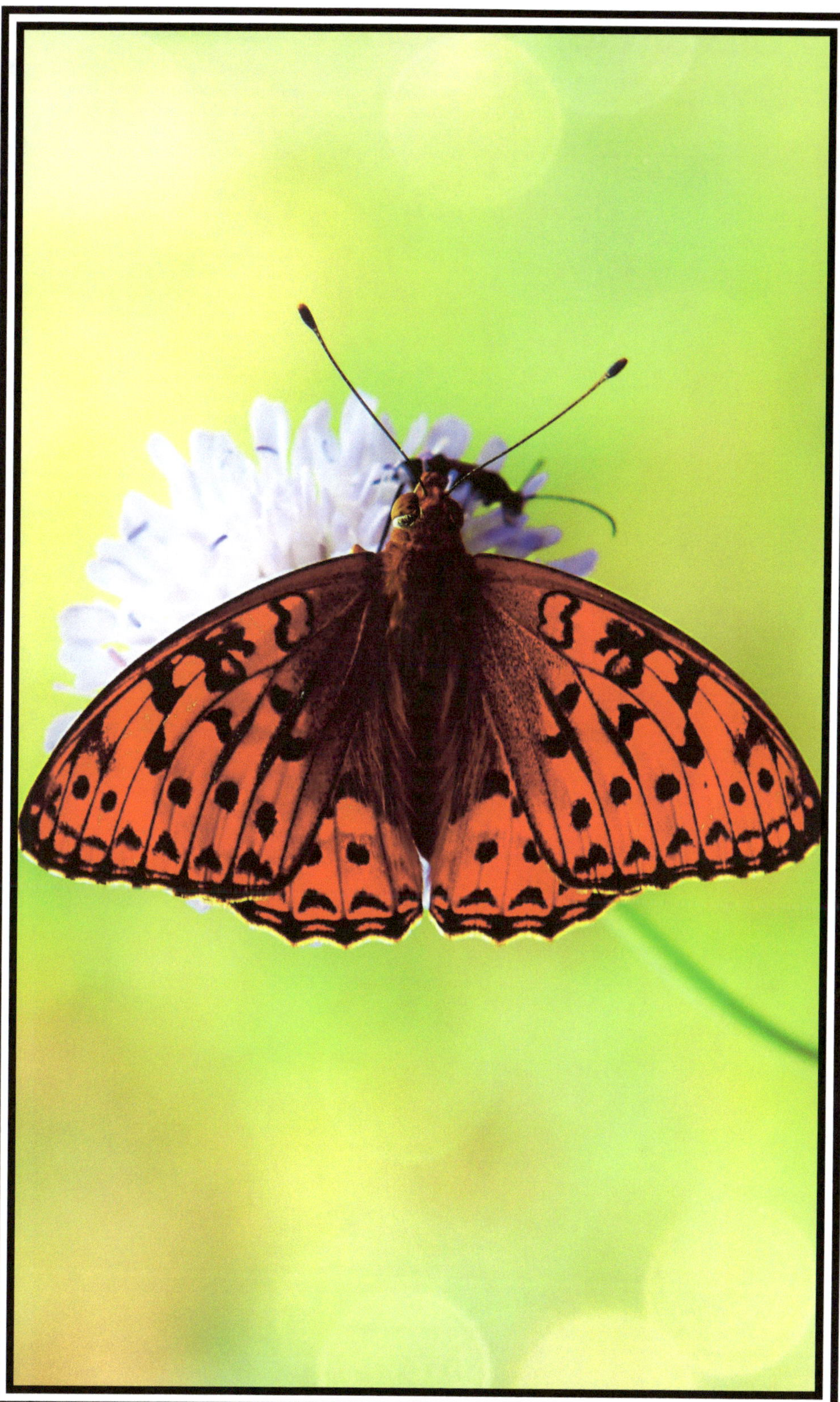

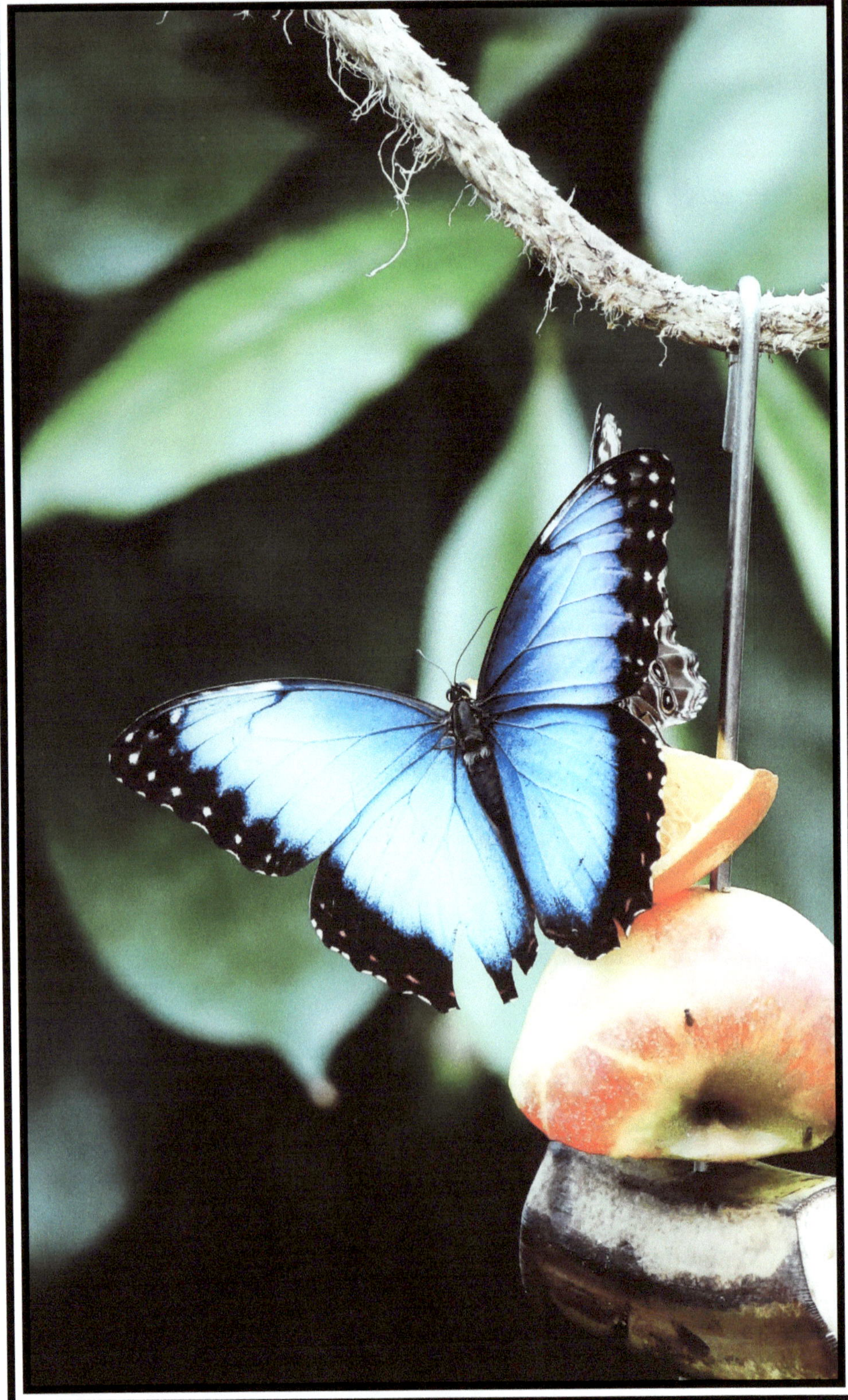

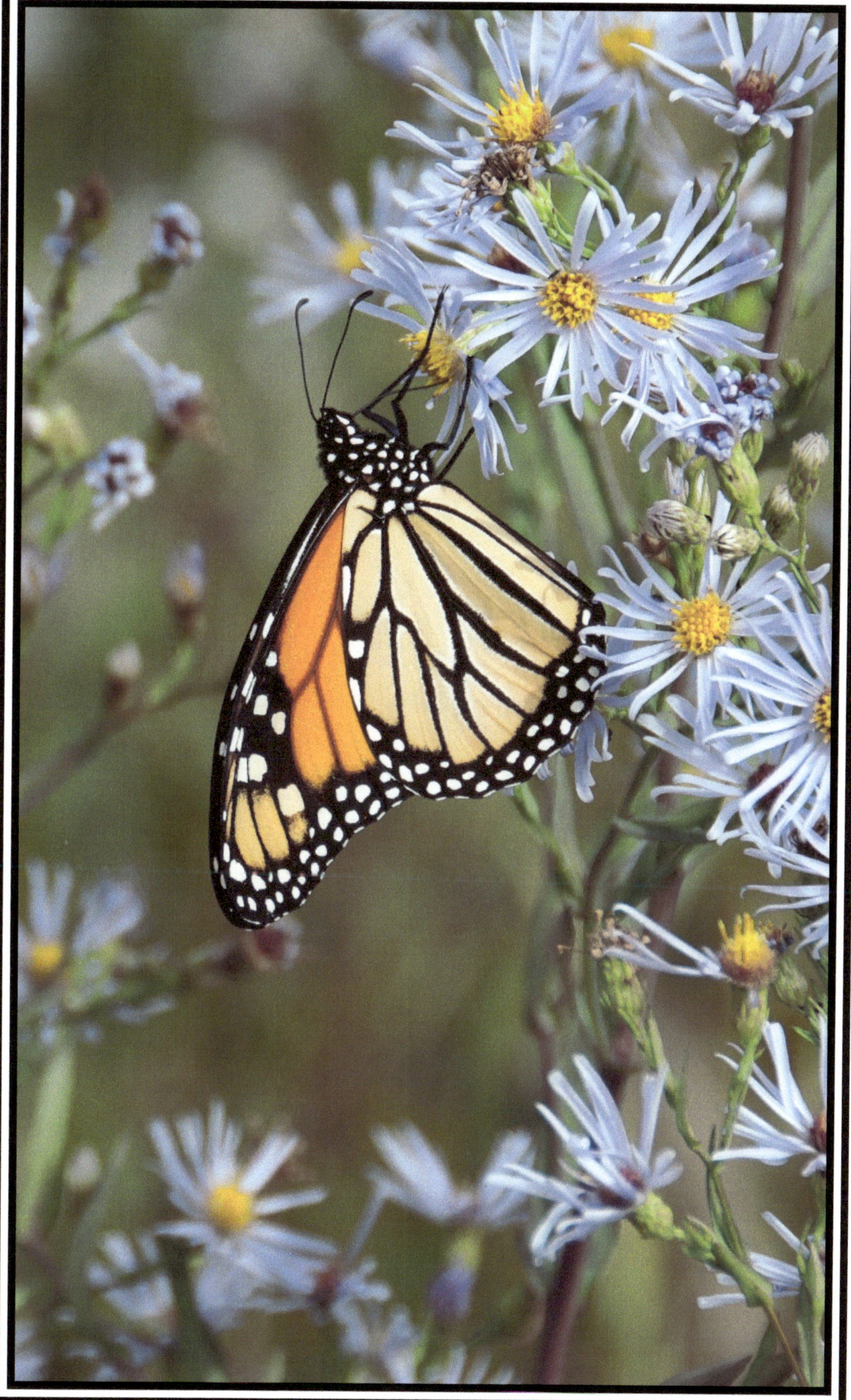

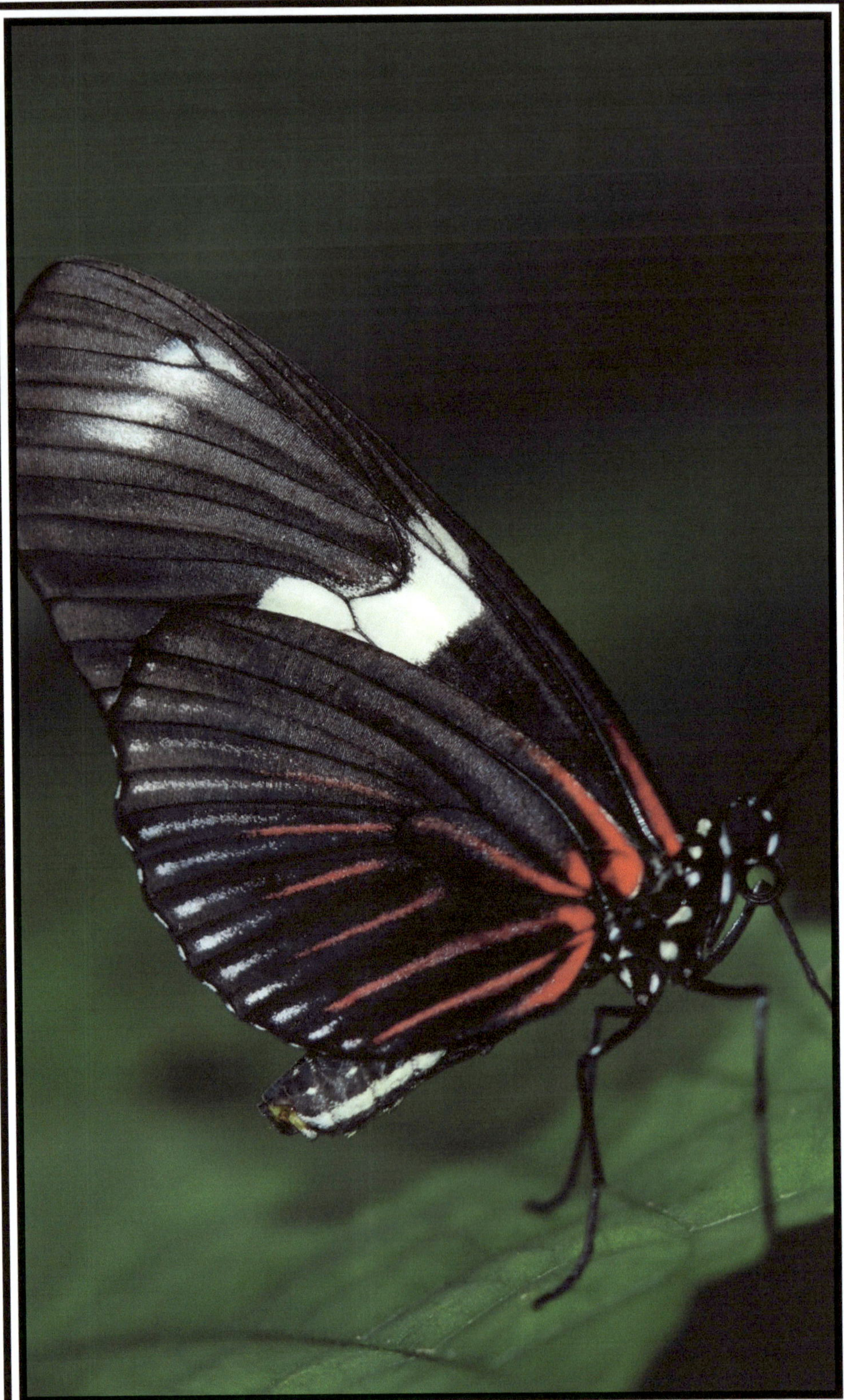

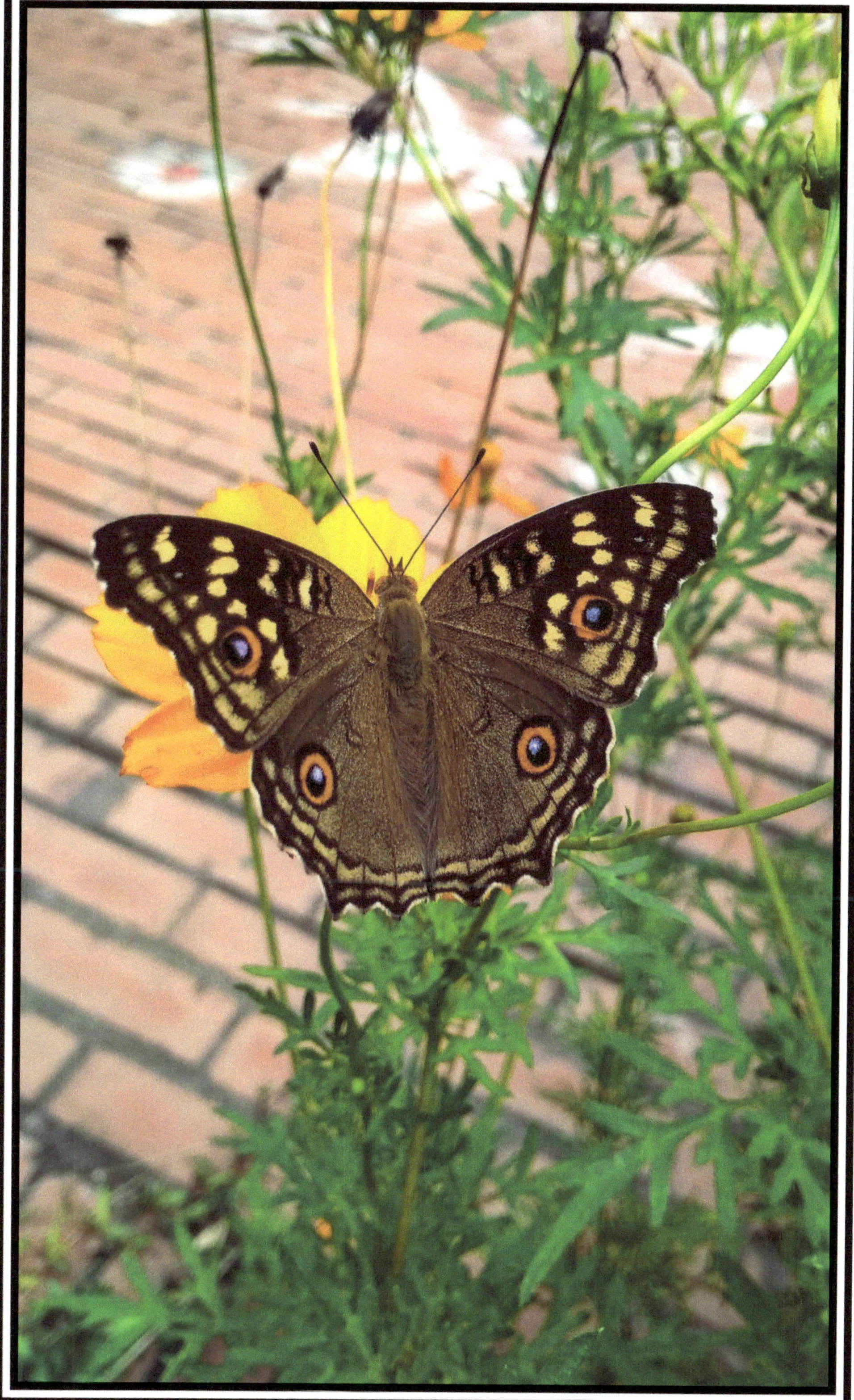

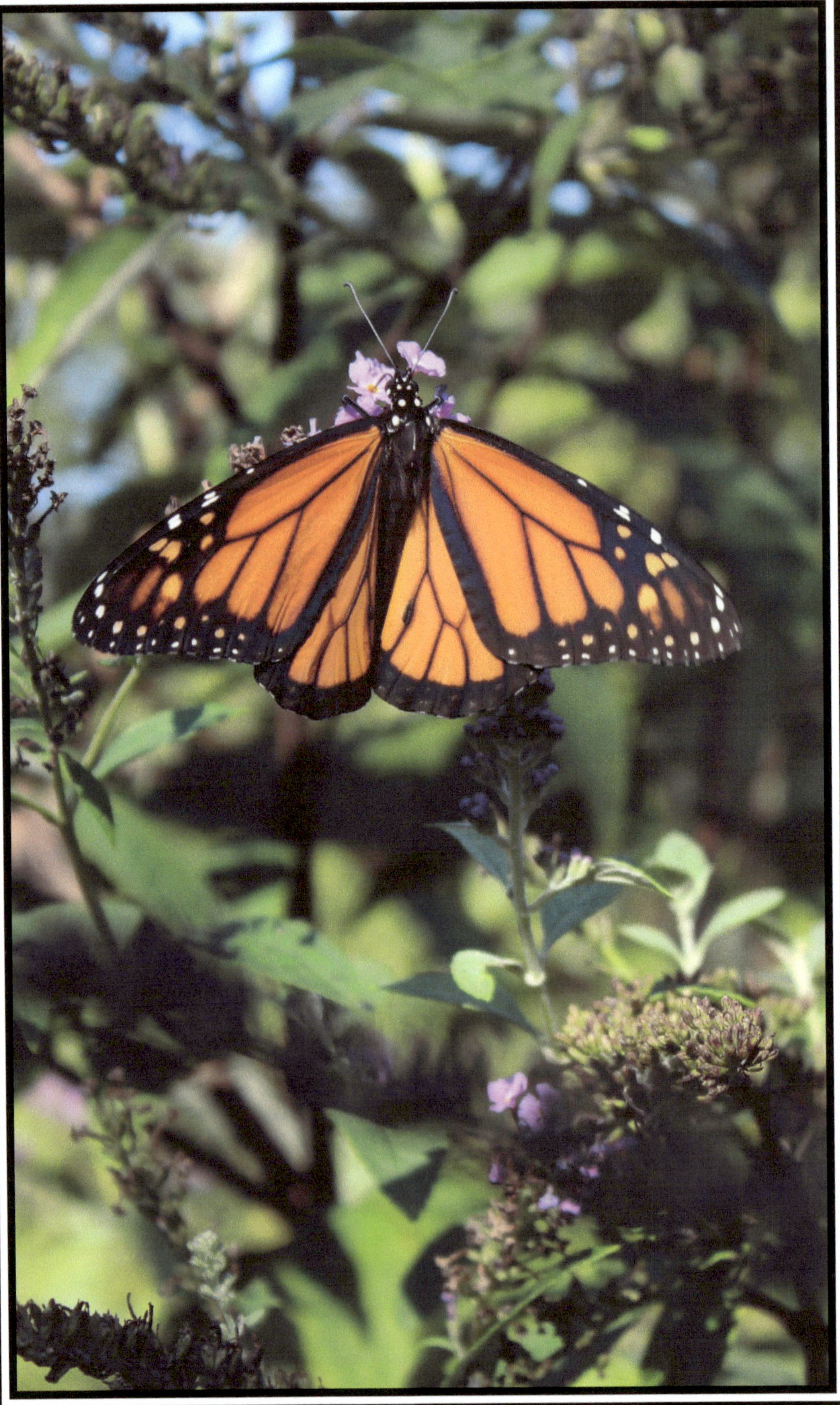

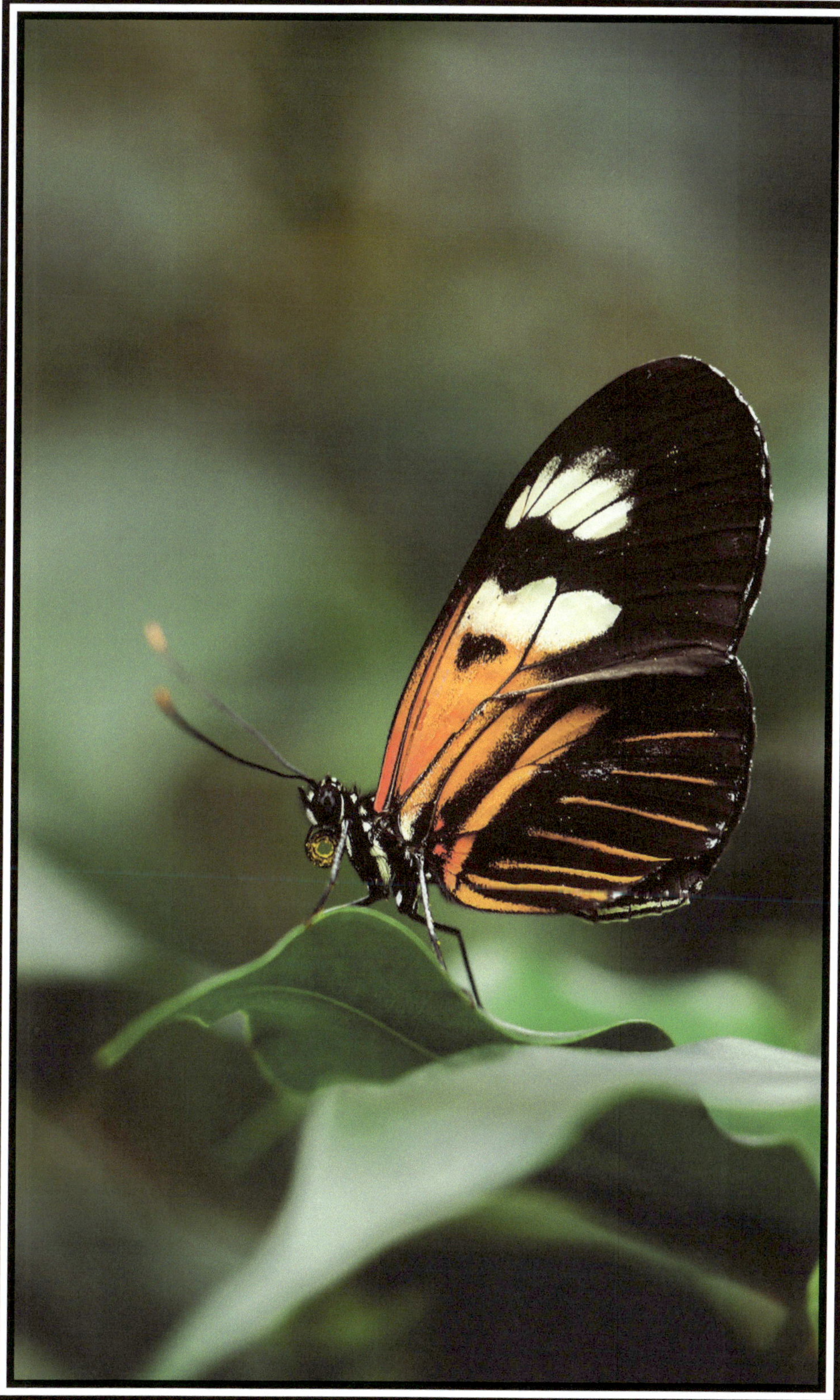

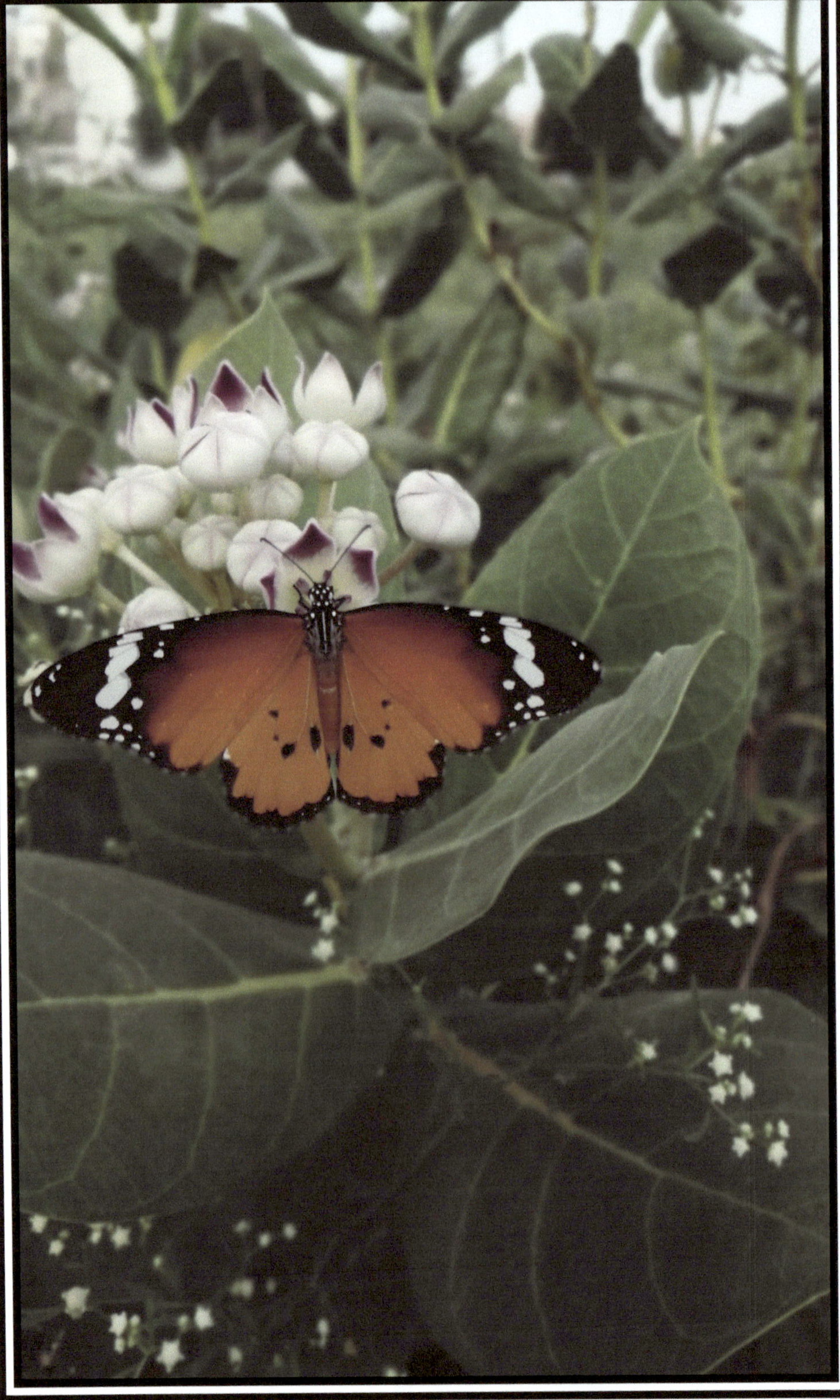

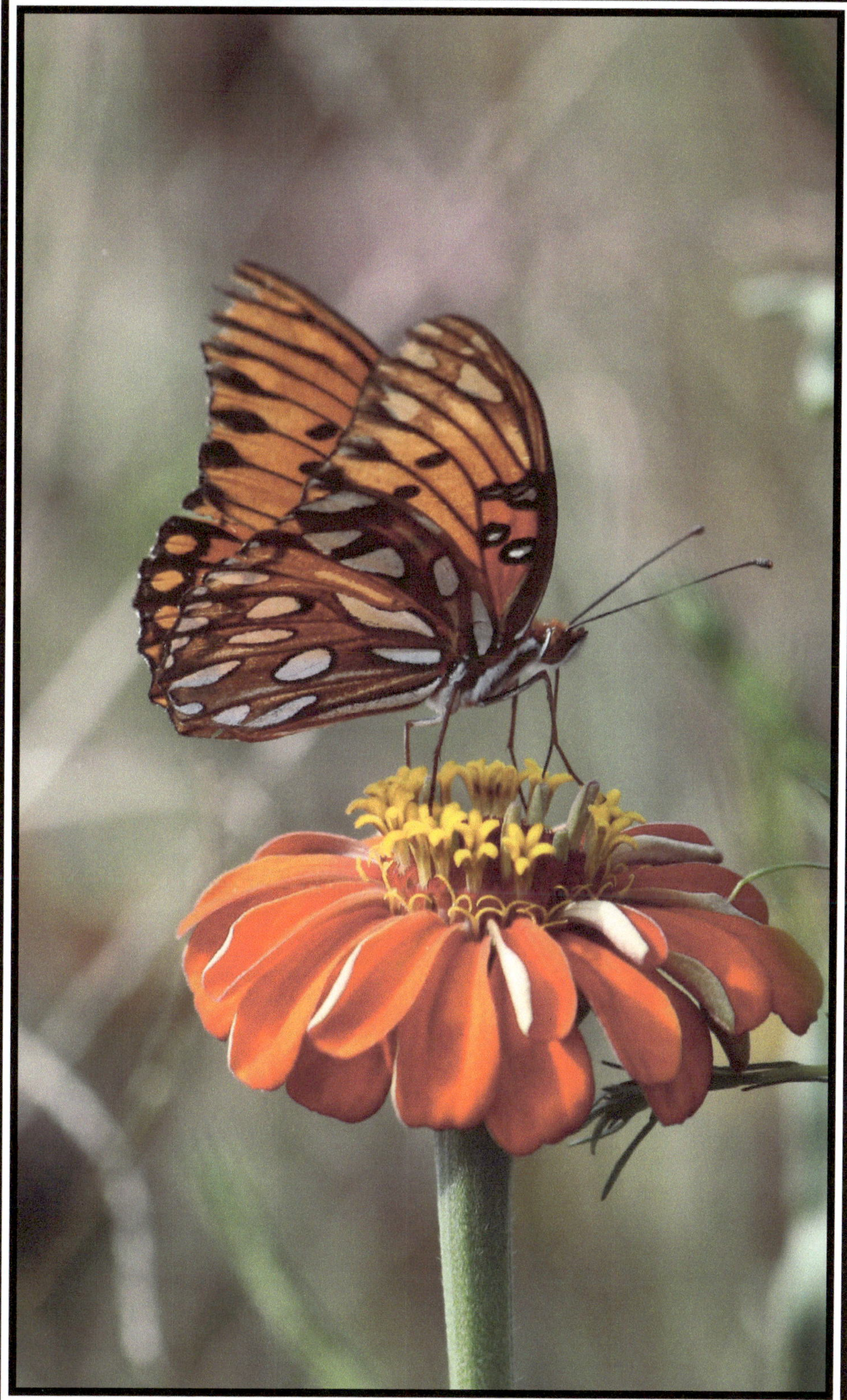

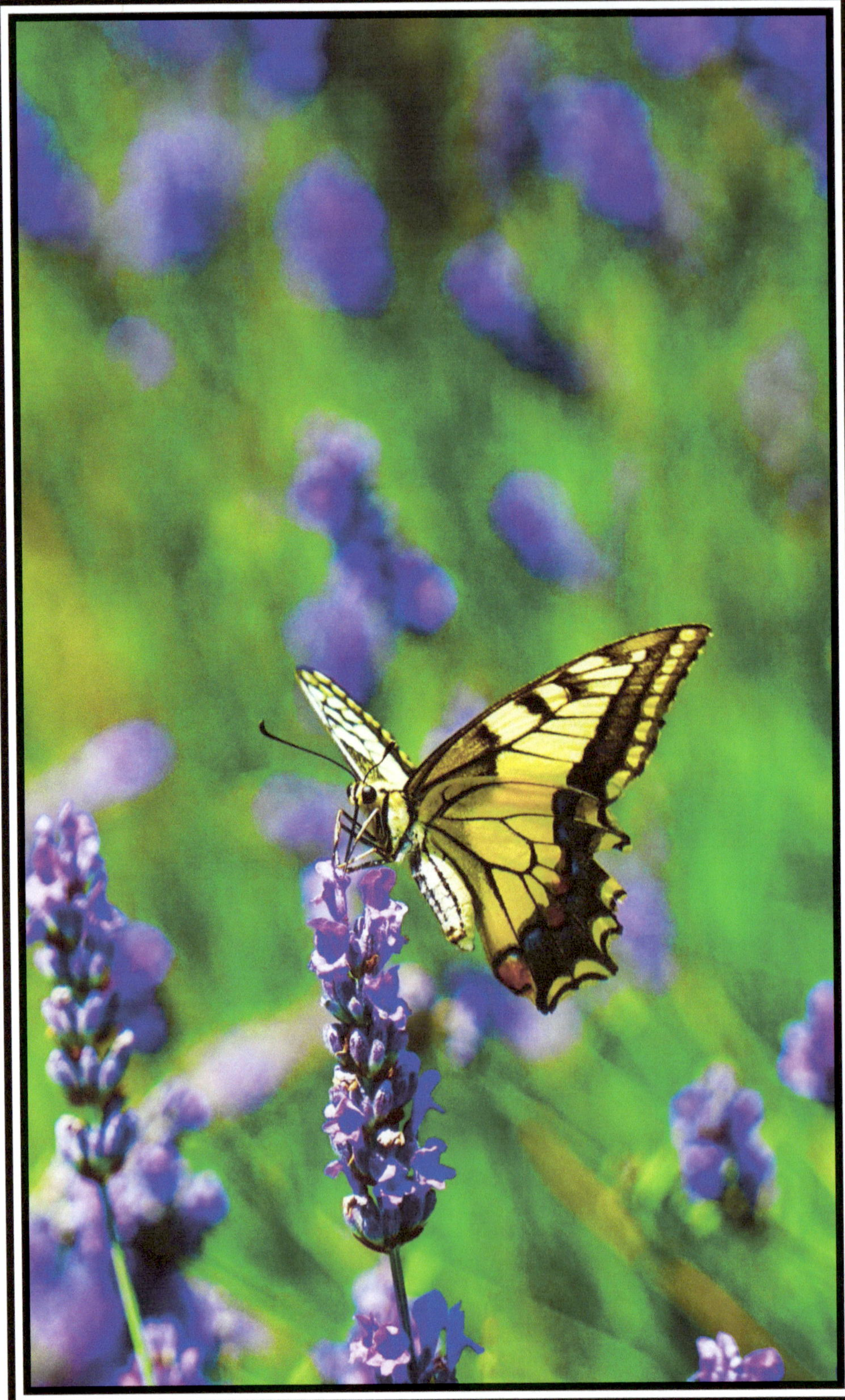

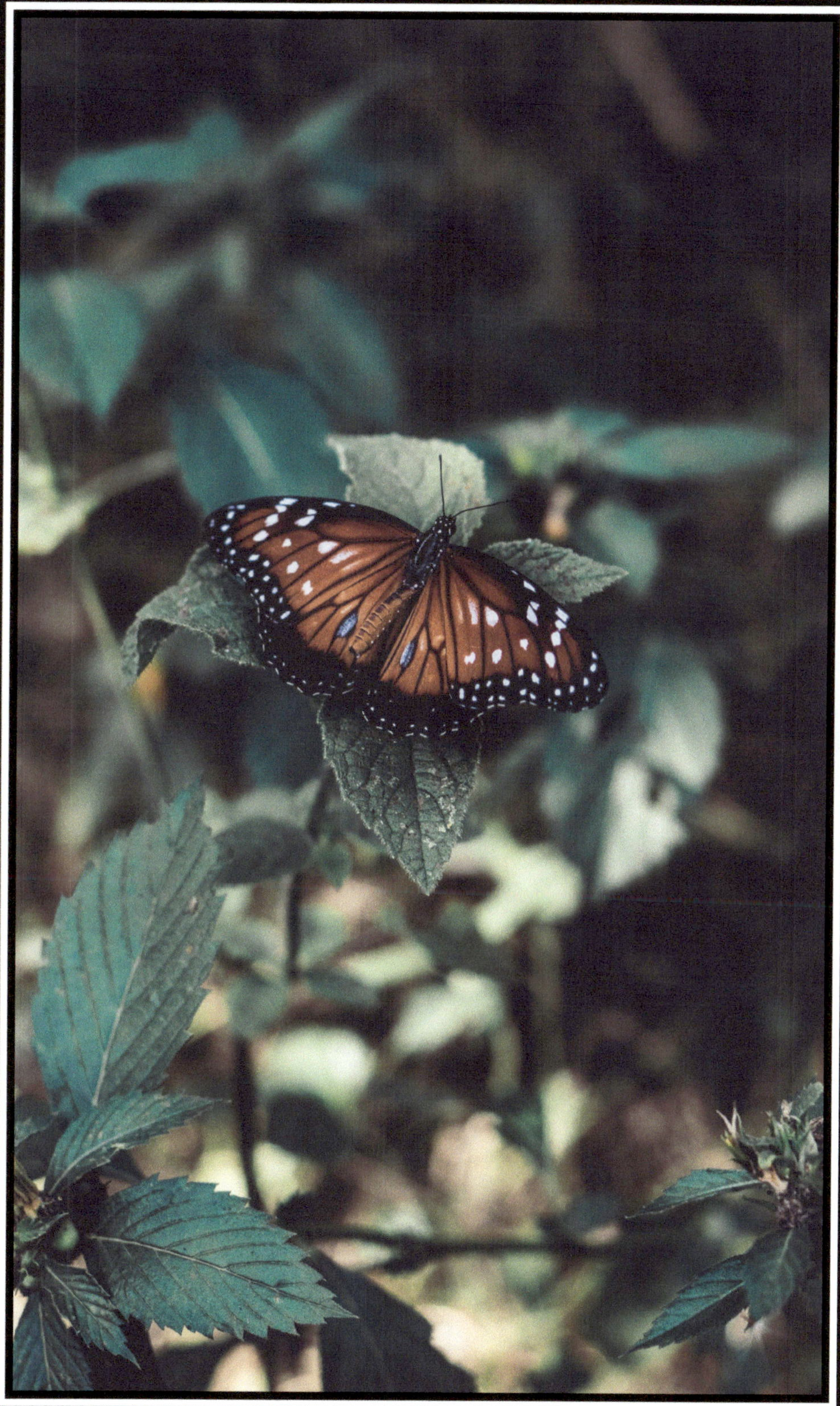

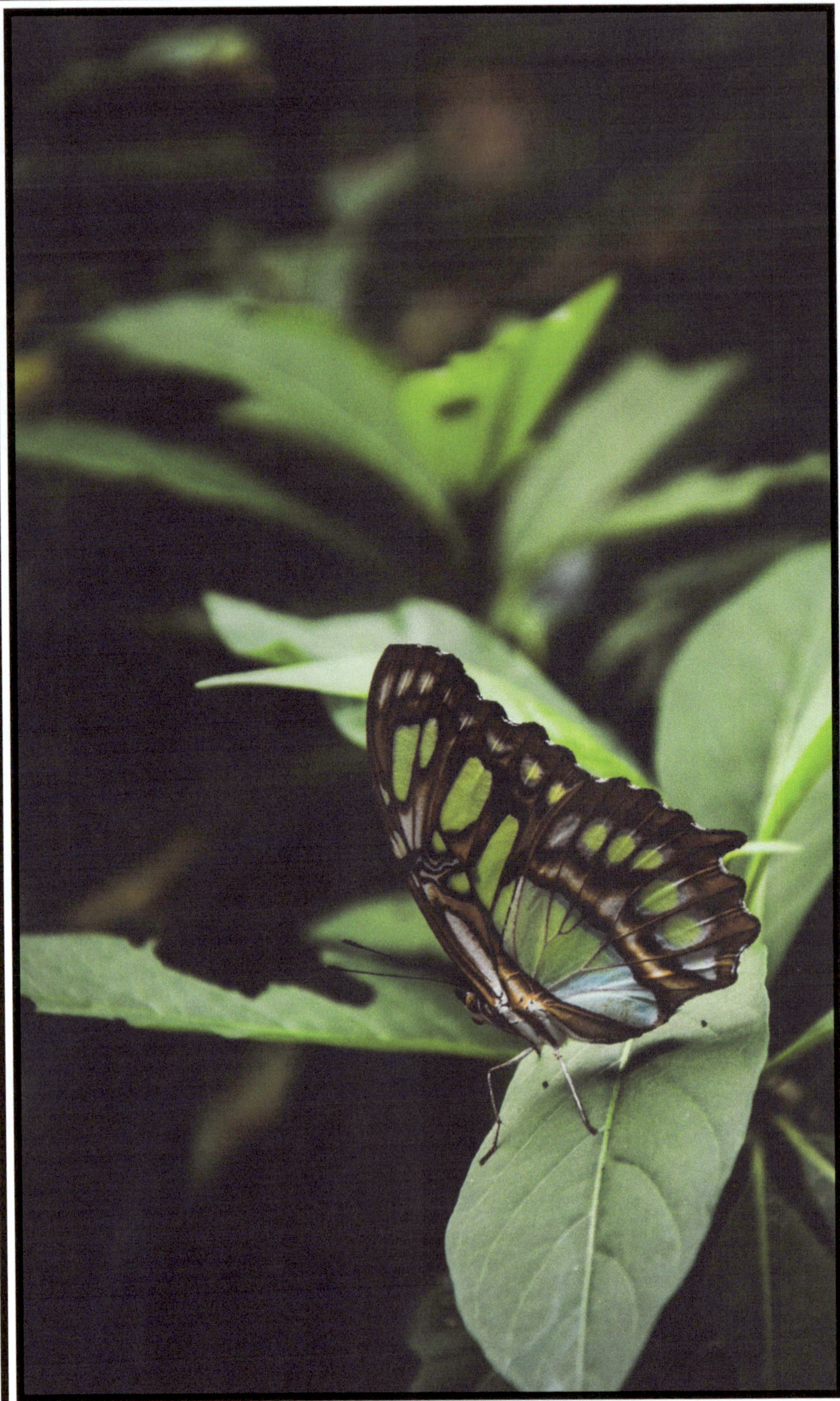

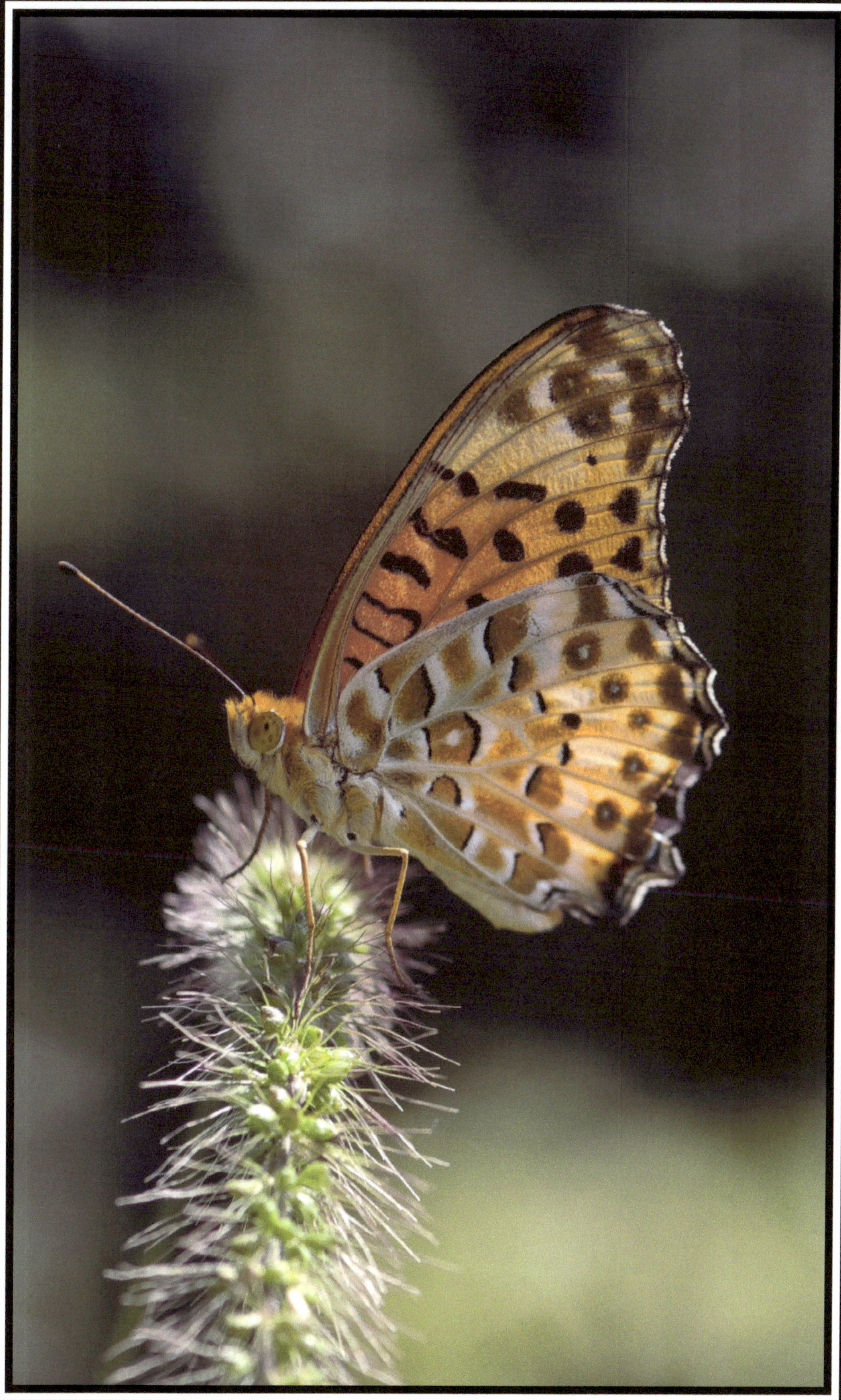

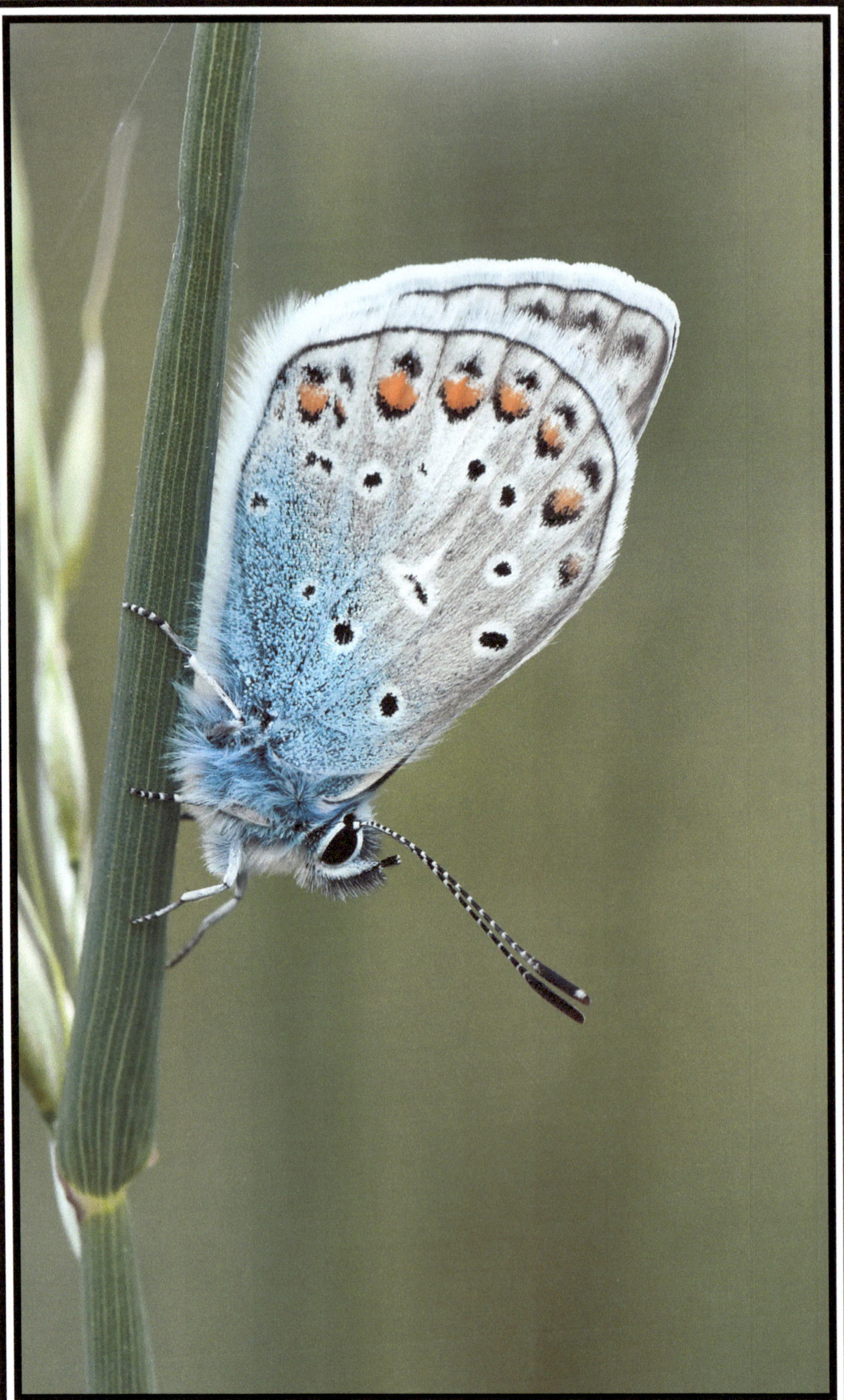

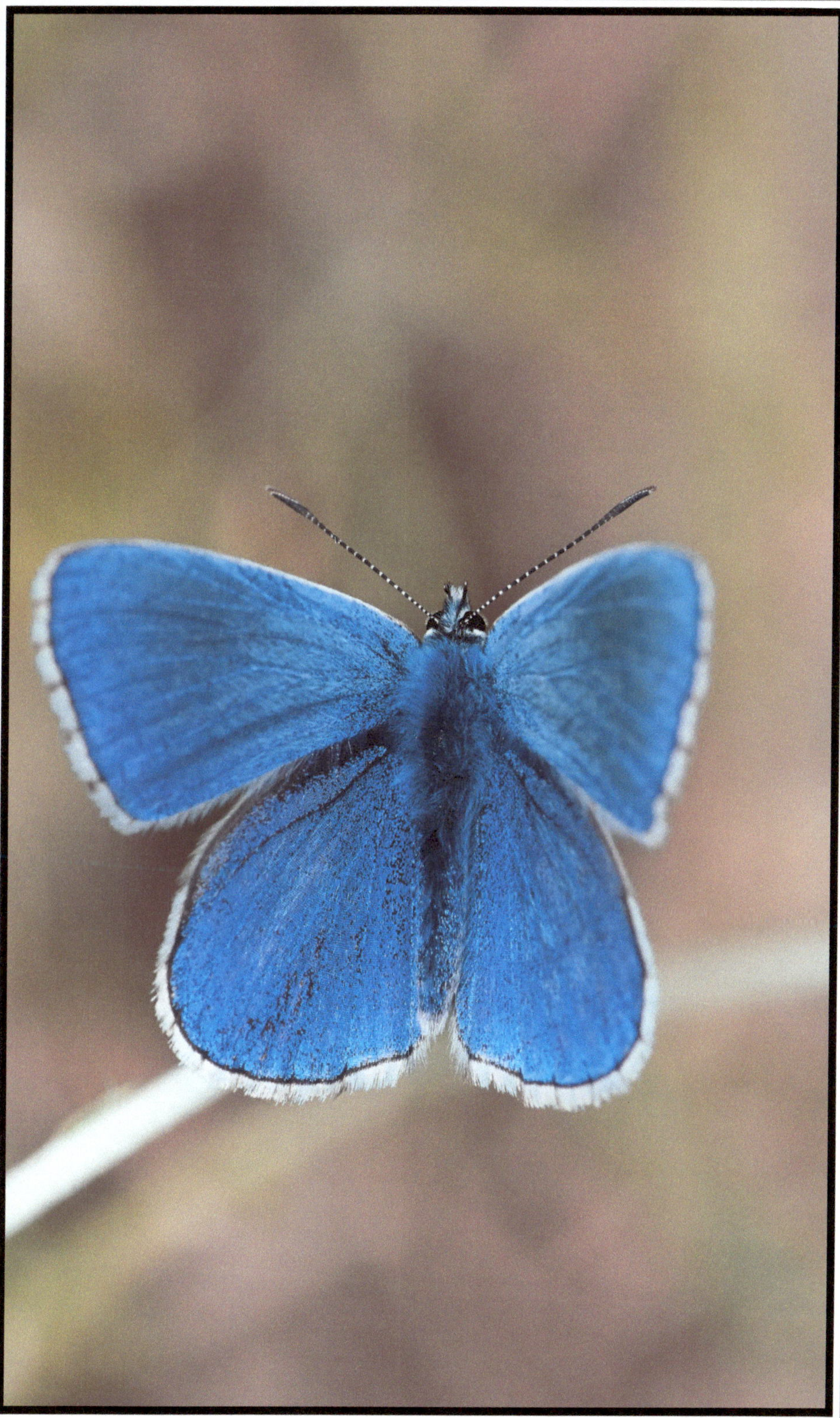

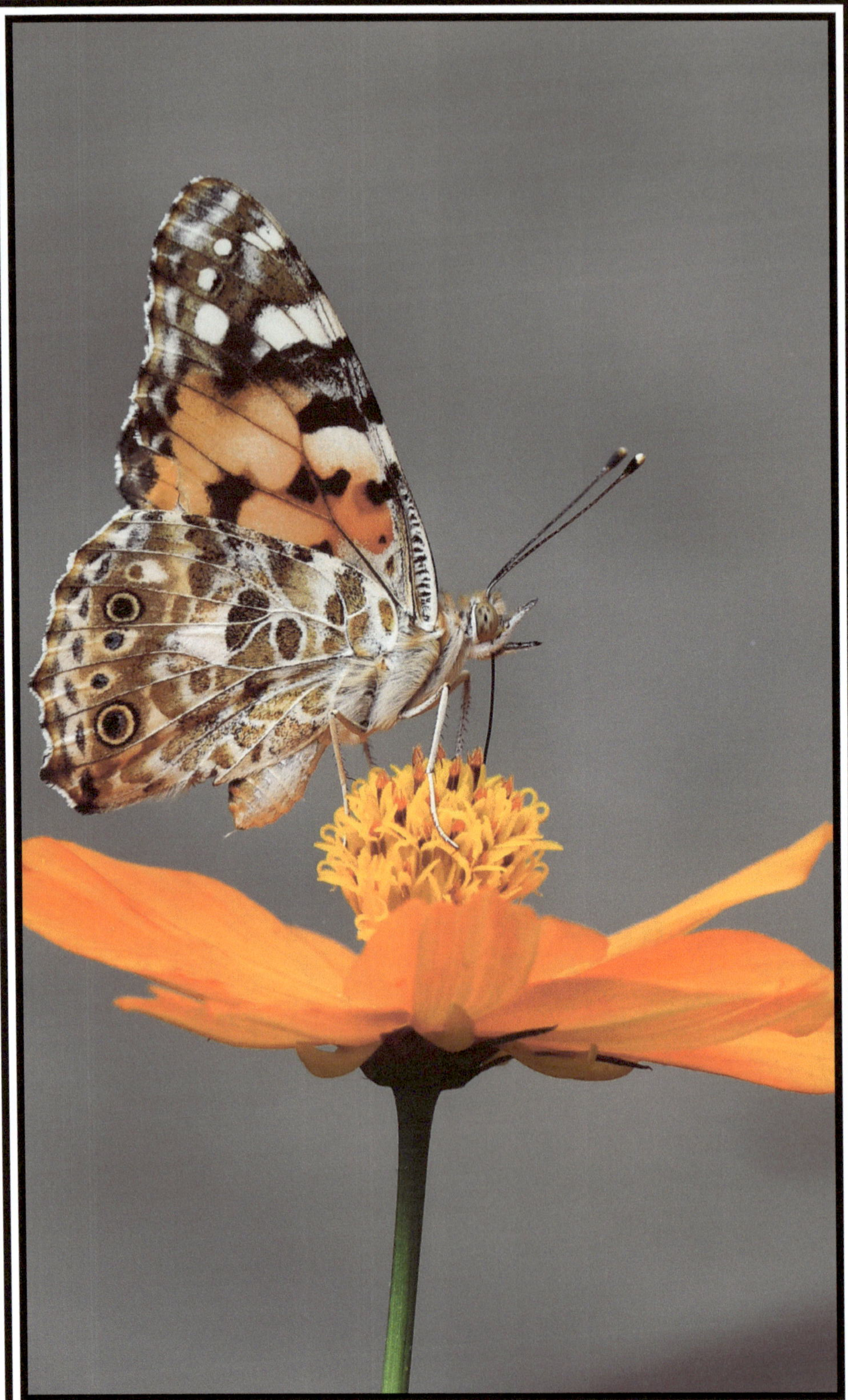

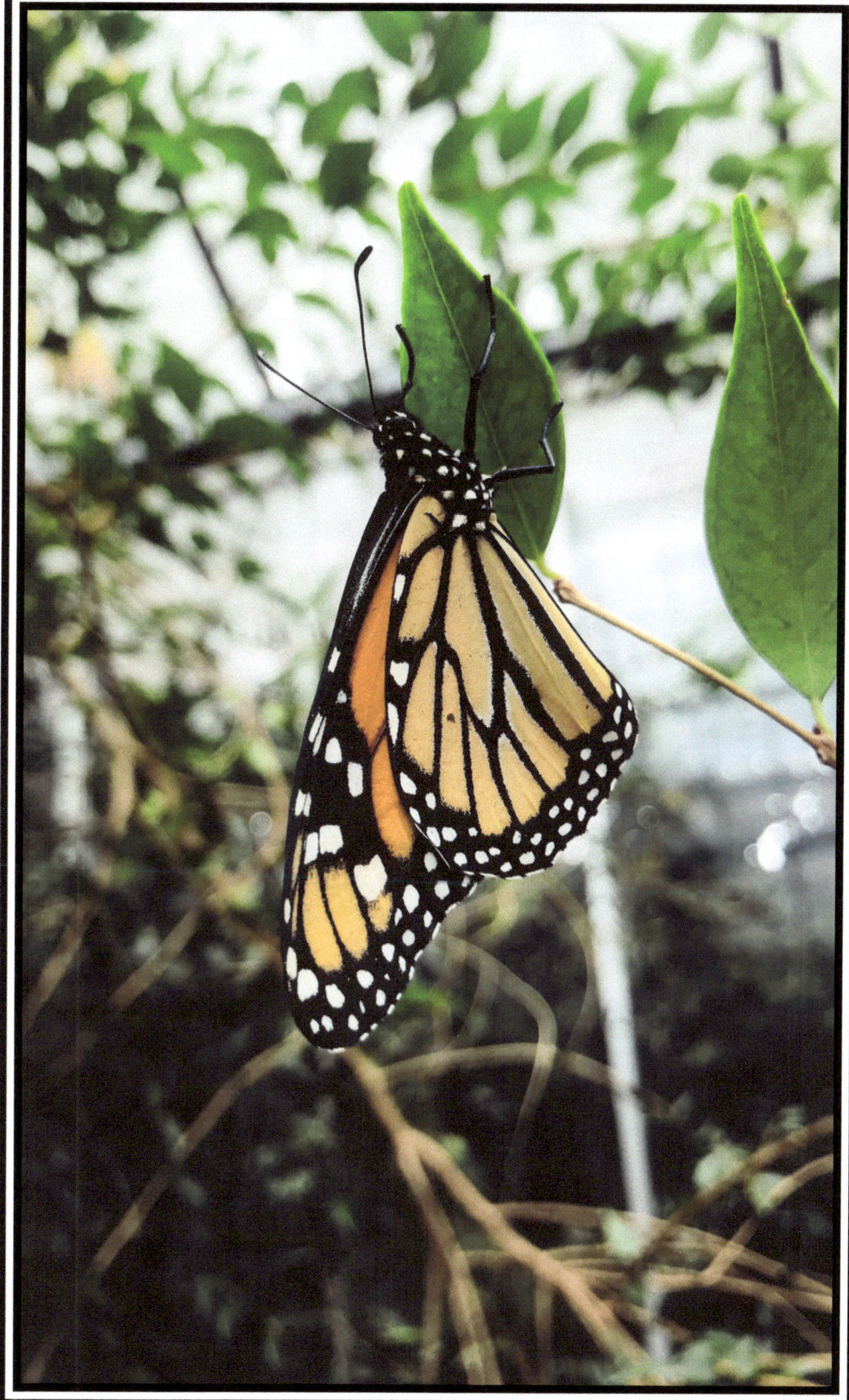